Authentic texts in foreign language teaching: theory and practice

**David Little
Seán Devitt
David Singleton**

Authentik

© 1988
Authentik Language Learning Resources Ltd
Dublin

ISBN 1 871730 00 7

Foreword

Ten years ago the idea of a communicative approach to language teaching was still a novelty. Some teachers seized on it eagerly, seeing in it an opportunity to give new purpose to their classes and new impetus to their pupils. Others received it with scepticism, doubting whether it could really succeed where other much-vaunted approaches and methods had so manifestly failed. Nowadays major victories are claimed for the communicative approach in every area of language teaching, and it is a rare teacher who will declare him- or herself to be anti-communicative.

The communicative approach has no single source and certainly exists in no single version. Inevitably, in the process of transmission the principles which provide its underpinning have often been diluted and sometimes been lost sight of; and many language teachers who claim to follow the communicative approach in their classroom would find it difficult to explain exactly what it consists of. Such has been the success of the missionaries who some fifteen years ago set out to convert the language teaching world to the communicative approach that in perhaps the majority of language classrooms it is manifested at least in the form of two lowest common denominators: emphasis on the spoken language and use of authentic texts. Often, however, these two phenomena are almost wholly divorced from one another in methodology and in the way classes are structured.

It is the purpose of this book to re-examine some of the basic principles on which the communicative approach is founded, to show why authentic texts should be at the centre of the foreign language learning process, and to propose ways in which teachers can broaden their scope for creative pedagogical initiatives. The book is the first in a series of publications that Authentik intends to bring out over the next few years in order to provide more support for teachers and learners using the *Authentik* newspapers and cassettes. In the autumn of 1989 we shall publish the first part of a manual for language learners, which will be designed to promote the development of greater autonomy in language learning. The second and third parts of the manual are scheduled to appear in the autumn of 1991.

The present book is divided into four chapters, two of them theoretical in their orientation and two of them more practical. Chapter 1 briefly reviews some of the principal findings of language acquisition research and begins to consider what implications they have for language teaching. Chapter 2 goes on to examine the basic principles of communicative language teaching, with particular reference to the use of authentic texts. Chapter 3 then offers a practical working out of these principles in the form of a battery of exercise types for use with authentic texts. Finally, Chapter 4 analyses the tasks set in Leaving Certificate examinations and relates them to the exercise types presented in Chapter 3. There are suggestions for further reading at the end of each chapter.

The book was conceived jointly by the three authors. Seán Devitt drafted sections 1 and 2 of Chapter 1 and Chapter 4; David Singleton drafted sections 3 and 4 of Chapter 1; and David Little drafted Chapters 2 and 3 and acted as editor for the book as a whole.

We are glad to acknowledge our debt to the editors of the three editions of *Authentik* and the groups of practising teachers who help them month by month in the selection of materials and the devising of exercises: their efforts gave us a rich source of examples to draw on. We are also glad to acknowledge our gratitude to the newspaper and magazine publishers who so generously allow us to reproduce their copyright material in *Authentik*.

David Little
Seán Devitt
David Singleton

Dublin
November 1988

Contents

Chapter 1

Language acquisition

Language acquisition research and language teaching

This chapter summarizes some of the principal findings of research into first and second language acquisition. The importance of such findings for the development of language teaching methodology cannot easily be exaggerated. After all, measures designed to assist the learning of foreign languages in a classroom environment are more likely to be successful if they take account of what we know about the mechanisms involved.

"Acquisition" and "learning"

The acquisition of a first language is almost by definition a natural process; and much of the research into second language acquisition has focussed on learning that has taken place outside a formal educational environment. However, research findings do not justify a hard and fast distinction between what is sometimes called "naturalistic" language acquisition on the one hand and the process of learning that goes on in a foreign language classroom on the other. Accordingly we use "acquisition" and "learning" interchangeably.

"Second" and "foreign" languages

It is sometimes useful to distinguish between "second" and "foreign" languages as between languages that respectively are and are not spoken in the community of which the learner is (at least temporarily) a member. However, in what follows "second language acquisition" should always be taken to refer to the learning of "foreign" as well as "second" languages.

1.1 Stages and natural orders in the acquisition of first and second languages

Earliest stages of L1 acquisition

Research has shown that the earliest stages of first language acquisition are remarkably similar for children the world over, irrespective of the particular language they happen to be acquiring. Typically a child reaches the cooing stage between 1 and 4 months, moves on to the babbling stage between 4 and 8 months, and begins to produce its first words at any time between 9 and 18 months. Gradually it begins to combine words, first as pairs of utterances, then as single utterances made up of two words. The two-word stage, which is reached between 18 and 24 months, is characterized by a rapid growth in vocabulary. Hitherto most of the words acquired were nouns; now verbs become much more frequent.

Patterns of acquisition differ from language to language

From the two-word stage onwards patterns of development differ significantly from language to language. Children acquiring English, for example, do not use any morphological markers (i.e. endings) on either nouns or verbs at the two-word stage; however, from very early in this stage they use correct English word order. This reflects the fact that word order is more important than morphology in establishing the relations between the components of utterances in English. By contrast, children acquiring the Romance languages do not show the same consistency in word order at the two-word stage; this is perhaps due to the fact that in their spoken form the Romance languages allow much freer word order than English. In Turkish the relations between the components of utterances are marked by morphology (the forms words take) rather than by word order; accordingly, morphology is acquired early. Children acquiring Polish, a highly inflected language, seem to acquire tense and aspect in verbs simultaneously, earlier and more quickly than children acquiring other languages. Polish also has an elaborate case system for nouns, and children in the third month of the two-word stage can already use the accusative, genitive and vocative cases (as well as the nominative, which is the first form to be acquired) with almost total accuracy. What all this amounts to is that the features of their mother tongue that children acquire earliest tend to be those on which successful communication crucially depends.

Natural orders in the acquisition of morphological features: English as L1

Although languages differ from one another as regards the stage at which children start to acquire morphology, research has shown that within a particular language all children follow a similar *route*, though the *rate* of acquisition may differ from child to child. In other words, there seems to be a natural order for the acquisition of morphological features. The pioneering work done in this area by Roger Brown suggested, for example, that in English the morphology of verbs tends to be mastered in the order: present progressive (*-ing*); irregular past tense (e.g. *went, brought*) and uncontractible copula (*am, is*); regular past tense (i.e. *-t, -d, -ed*); third person singular (*-s*) and third person irregular (e.g. *has, is*); uncontractible auxiliary (*is, am*), contractible copula (*is, am*), contractible auxiliary (*is, am*). Research dealing with other languages has shown that their morphology is also acquired in a relatively fixed order.

Natural orders in the acquisition of morphological features: English as L2

Studies in second language acquisition were much slower to start than those in first language acquisition, but once started they rapidly gained an impetus of their own. One of the areas that has attracted most attention has been the acquisition of the morphology of English. The major findings indicate that, irrespective of their linguistic background, children and adults acquiring English as a second language "naturalistically" (i.e. without the benefit of formal instruction), acquire English morphology in a relatively stable order, though the order differs from that shown by children acquiring English as a first language. It must be admitted, however, that these findings and the research methodology underlying them are not without their critics. Less vulnerable to criticism are the studies which have investigated the development of syntactic structures such as negation and interrogation. They have revealed that learners of English as a second language, whatever their native language background, pass through very similar stages on their way to acquiring the structures in question, and that these stages resemble those passed through by children acquiring English as a first language.

The few studies of the acquisition of English as a second language that have been carried out in the classroom show similar routes of development to those found in studies of acquisition in natural environments. The data, however, are very limited; so that while they are indicative of trends, they must be treated with caution until confirmed (or disconfirmed) by other studies.

Acquisition of English as L2 in the classroom

Data for the acquisition of French as a second language are less complete than for English. However, one of the present authors found that his two subjects (English-speaking girls aged 11 and 8 studied during a 5-month period of residence in France) followed a definite path in acquiring the verbal system, and his findings are consistent with those of researchers in Canada who have examined the acquisition of the French verbal system in immersion classrooms. Research into the acquisition of the verbal system by learners of German shows a similar stability in its pattern of development.

Natural orders in the acquisition of French and German as L2

To sum up: there is ample and growing evidence that second as well as first language acquisition follows relatively fixed routes of development that fall into clearly marked stages; and there is some evidence that this applies as much to classroom as to "naturalistic" learners of second languages. There is also, however, equally ample evidence of variability in the speed at which learners progress along these routes. Clearly there is no fixed rate at which the successive stages are reached, and there can be no suggestion that the whole second language acquisition process is characterized by stable sequences - such a suggestion would be extremely difficult to sustain in relation to, for example, vocabulary acquisition or the development of the capacity to fit utterances to an increasing variety of contexts.

Summary of findings on routes and rates of L1 and L2 development

These research findings should not be taken to

General implications of these findings

imply that the process of language acquisition is one over which we can have no control; but neither should we assume that language teaching should seek to follow closely the natural route(s) of acquisition. For one thing, the routes are not yet entirely clear; for another, it seems that "natural orders" are a product of internal mental processes rather than of the environment. At the same time, the context in which acquisition occurs plays a central role in determining its success. It is to this aspect of language acquisition that we now turn.

1.2 The context of language acquisition

The role of input and communication in L1 acquisition

The evidence for relatively fixed stages and natural orders in language acquisition is gleaned from an analysis of learners' linguistic output, i.e. the language they speak or write. In our summary of language acquisition research we have so far made no mention of input, i.e. the language spoken to the child by the parent or caretaker, or to the second language learner by native speakers or teachers. Neither have we mentioned the communication jointly created by the learner and his or her interlocutor. Yet an understanding of these aspects of the context in which language acquisition takes place is fundamental if we are ever to get a full picture of the process.

Example: a typical dialogue

The following typical dialogue illustrates how a child at the one-word stage has already acquired an understanding of discourse structure.

Child:	Mammy! Mammy!
Mother:	Yes, dear, what is it?
Child:	Liga!
Mother:	Oh, you poor darling! Your shoe has fallen into the Liga.

This conversation has the following "vertical" structure:

Child:	Nomination.
Mother:	Acknowledgement.
	Elicitation of topic for comment.
Child:	Nomination of topic.
Mother:	Comment on topic.

"Vertical" and "horizontal" structures in language acquisition

The important things to note here are: (i) that the child has acquired the "vertical" structure of conversation before being able to combine words "horizontally" - in other words, it knows how the successive components of a conversation hold together but cannot yet give them full syntactic embodiment; and (ii) that the mother provides the model for the "horizontal" structuring of language. Language is not acquired in a vacuum but is laid down on previously developed structures of interaction. Before reaching the "linguistic" period, the child gradually builds up with its parents or caretakers a knowledge of the rules of interaction and a knowledge of the world. These two kinds of knowledge provide a "scaffolding" which shapes the "vertical" structure of discourse; within it the parent or caretaker is constantly providing the child with a model for the "horizontal" structure. The child begins its linguistic participation in interaction by incorporating parts of the model, then gradually becomes independent of it.

World knowledge: adult and adolescent L2 learners compared with children acquiring L1

We have seen that there are close similarities between first and second language acquisition in regard to the route by which learners acquire morphology. Might there not also be similarities in the use of "scaffolding" as a "vertical" framework for the acquisition of "horizontal" structures? Clearly, adolescent or adult second language learners are in a very different situation from that of the child learning its first language. Because they have a much greater experience of the world, they possess a much wider range of potential conversational topics, and it is not natural for their conversations to be limited to the here and now, as the conversations of small children usually are. In the early stages it is often difficult for adolescent or adult second language learners to establish precisely what aspects of their world knowledge need to be activated. This can cause frequent breakdown in communication, and because it seems to impose cognitive inferiority on the learner vis-à-vis the native speaker, it can be a source of serious frustration.

Importance of exploiting L2 learners' world and discourse knowledge

However, it is possible to go a long way towards overcoming this difficulty by exploiting rather than ignoring the two types of knowledge that adolescents and adults bring with them to the language learning task: their knowledge of the world and their knowledge of how different types of discourse are structured. One possibility is to use authentic texts produced for native speakers. If they work with such texts from the earliest stages of language learning, it is not necessary for them to feel that they are regressing to an earlier stage of their cognitive development; on the contrary, they can become effective language users even at the beginning of the learning process.

The need to create an appropriate environment in the L2 classroom

Common sense dictates that in the language classroom we should try to create conditions for learning which are as close as possible to those of natural acquisition. Although this is widely recognized as an ideal, it is rejected by many as impracticable because of the constraints imposed by time and the physical situation of the classroom. But the danger is that if we ignore the natural contexts of language acquisition and by-pass the frameworks already available within the learner's experience, we may actually block the learning process.

Example: two texts produced by learners of French in Dublin schools

Here are two examples of texts produced by children learning French at school in Dublin. They illustrate how the pupils' knowledge of the world and their knowledge of how stories are written enabled them to free linguistic potential that might otherwise have gone unrecognized and unfulfilled. The first text is the work of four 13-year-old girls in their second year of learning French; the second was written by a 12-year-old boy

7

(from a different school) in his first year of learning French. In both cases the pupils had been given a jumble of French words taken from a newspaper article, had been asked to sort them into semantic clusters, and had then been invited to use the clusters to create a story.

Text produced by four 13-year-old girls

James Dean Septembre 1955: il habite en Bakersfield. Il aimé le cinema et à 24 ans il a allé en Californie et il entré le cinema. Il as très bien. Il ne porter pas uniforme, mais il preferè blue jeans et t-shirt. Les adolescents adorent James Dean et ses films, par example A l'Est d'Eden et Geant. Les années 80 le film "La Fureur de Vivre" tres populaire. 1987 dans le Ford Modèle 50 il a eu accident et il mouri. Il a eu trente-deux ans. Aujourd-hui il a symbole et célèbre salles de cinema et les adolescents et les adultes moderne aiment James Dean.

Text produced by 12-year-old boy

Hasard de mortel
Le Martine et Jean-Luc dans un caverne. Commencer un glisser et s'affaisser un caverne. "Il faut échapper" dire Martine. Voir homme vieux le glisser. "Il faut donner l'alerte" il dire. Arriver police. "Ils faut être mort" dire un. Enlever le police le glisser. Etre Martine et Jean-Luc être dans un état grave. Aller Jean-Luc et Martine hôpital. Ils être mort le Lendemain. Le lendemain être ensevelir.

Features of these learner texts

Many teachers would throw up their hands in horror at these texts because of the many errors they contain. But if we disregard the errors we cannot but be amazed at the pupils' achievement in using minimal linguistic means to communicate very interesting accounts of James Dean and of an imagined accident. Both texts have a clear "vertical" structure, in the sense in which that term was used above, yet their "horizontal" structure is "pragmatic" rather than "syntactic".

That is to say, it is made up of small rather than large chunks, which are articulated according to a topic-comment rather than a subject-predicate pattern; the relation between chunks is one of loose co-ordination rather than tight subordination; the ratio of nouns to verbs is low; and there is no use of morphology.

Purpose for which the texts were created: comprehension of authentic texts

It is important to note that the pupils created these texts not as ends in themselves but as a means of gaining access to an authentic text - in fact, the text which provided the words the pupils began with. They found the text easy to understand, which they almost certainly would not have done if they had not first created a scaffolding by exploiting their existing world and discourse knowledge. Furthermore, it would be possible for them to edit their texts into a form much closer to authentic French, using the original text as a model of the "horizontal" structure of French (i.e. the fully syntacticized language). These are issues to which we shall return in Chapter 2 and which will provide the essential underpinning for Chapters 3 and 4.

1.3 The influence of the mother tongue

Most obvious difference between L1 and L2 acquisition

We have already mentioned some differences between first and second language acquisition. However, we have not yet referred to the most obvious difference of all. Whereas the beginning first language learner (unless he or she is learning two parental languages simultaneously) has experience of just one language, the second language learner, by definition, has encountered at least two. Moreover, since the typical second language learner in Ireland begins the second language learning process only upon entering the formal education system, he or she has a well-developed mastery of the first language before coming into contact with the second. From what we know about human learning generally, it would be extraordinary if such second language learners' dealings with their new language were entirely uninfluenced by what they have already experienced of and in their mother tongue.

In fact, as any language teacher knows, the influence of a second language learner's first language on his or her progress and performance in the second is usually fairly readily apparent. Traditionally, this influence has been perceived in largely negative terms. References to it in language teaching manuals produced in the first half of this century and earlier tend to consist in warnings about the dangers of lapsing into "Anglicisms", in "rogues galleries" of "false friends" (i.e. deceptive cognates), etc.

This general attitude persisted through the period when "audio-lingual" methodology was dominant - that is, from the late 1950s to the early 1970s. The psychological assumptions on which audio-lingual courses (and the audio-visual courses which developed out of them) were based were essentially behaviourist in nature; chief among them was the assumption that language acquisition was a matter of "conditioning", of appropriate responses to stimuli being "reinforced" in one way or another until they became automatized as "habits". On this view, learning a second language consisted in the formation of a second set of habits, a process which would be "facilitated" by "positive transfer" where the new habits to be learned coincided with already established first language habits, but "inhibited" or "interfered with" by "negative transfer" where there were divergences between first language habits and target patterns. In principle, therefore, the behaviourist account recognized both the negative aspect and the positive aspect of cross-linguistic influence. However, because the principal preoccupation in language teaching circles was, not unnaturally, the eradication of error, in practice emphasis was placed on the "interference" problem. The response to this problem proposed at the time was to attempt to predict interference errors by means of a "contrastive analysis" of the native and target systems and to forestall such errors by intensively drilling those parts of the

Influence of L1 on L2 development and performance

Audio-lingual methodology saw L2 learning as habit formation

Positive and negative transfer and interference

target language which showed marked differences from the learners' first language.

Shortcomings of contrastive analysis

The success of contrastive analysis was somewhat mixed. One major problem with it was its failure to recognize the above-discussed fact that many aspects of second language development seem closely to resemble aspects of first language development and are not directly or uniquely relatable to cross-linguistic influence; errors of a "developmental" kind were thus simply not predicted by contrastive analysis. Another was its association with the behaviourist account of language learning, which was increasingly under attack. In sum, there was widespread disillusionment with contrastive analysis in the 1970s - a disillusionment which in some circles led to claims that the cross-linguistic dimension of second language learning was of little or no significance.

New approaches to cross-linguistic influence

A clearly more sensible response was that of those researchers who sought to decouple the notion of cross-linguistic influence from the behaviourist view of language learning and to explore ways in which this notion could be integrated into accounts of second language learning which gave full weight to the active, creative role of the learner's internal processing mechanisms and communication strategies. Among the many interesting findings of research generated by this particular optique are the following:

(i) Difficulties arising from differences between the first and the second language system may move the learner to avoid using problematic structures in order not to produce errors.

(ii) Where a second language learner does use an element derived from his or her first language, this may be a more or less deliberate ploy to cover gaps in his or her second language knowledge; if such a strategy works in communication terms, the "borrowed" element may be incorporated into the learner's version of the target language.

(iii)   The degree to which second language learners
        will be inclined to draw on first language knowl-
        edge depends on how closely they perceive
        their second language to be related to their
        first; the corollary of this would seem to be that
        the greater the second language learner's re-
        course to first language knowledge, the more
        likely such tapping of mother tongue knowl-
        edge is to yield communicatively efficient out-
        comes.

(iv)   Second language learners' perceptions of simi-
        larities and differences between their first and
        second languages can be sharpened by certain
        kinds of classroom activities; the resultant
        heightened linguistic sensitivity can be helpful
        in dealing with second language difficulties.

(v)   First language influence appears to interact
        with developmental factors and, depending on
        the nature of the influence, may delay but may
        also accelerate progress through natural devel-
        opmental stages.

Nowadays a more positive attitude to the cross-linguistic factor in L2 learning seems appropriate

The effect of such findings is to allow the cross-linguistic factor in second language learning and performance to be seen in a rather more positive light - in terms not of inadequate conditioning, but rather of strategic avoidance and gap-filling, of linguistic sensitivity and of a normal, perhaps inevitable, dimension to the second language developmental process. There have always been linguists who have claimed that it is actually *through* our first language knowledge that we gain entry into a second language. Whether or not this proposition is literally true, it is now indisputable that there are circumstances and respects in which the role of the first language in second language acquisition and use is anything but negative. One very good example of the positive role of cross-linguistic influence, and one which is highly relevant in the present context, is the way in which the general meaning of an authentic foreign language text can often be understood by people with little or no knowledge of the language in question, simply on the basis of cognate recognition.

1.4 Attitude and motivation in second language learning

Importance of attitude in L2 learning

Another major difference between the child in the early stages of acquiring his or her mother tongue and the child or adolescent learning a second language at school is that the latter is at a stage of cognitive development that enables him or her to form an attitude towards the learning task in question, whereas this can hardly be said of the former. Indeed, the baby acquiring his or her first language is not even aware of a learning task. Very young children acquiring a second language "naturalistically" may also have a rather limited awareness of a language learning process as opposed to or distinct from their efforts to engage in communication through the second language. However, children learning a second language at school - whether or not under a "communicative" regime - perceive that language from the outset as having roughly the same status as other subjects on the timetable. This means that they see it as likely to make roughly the same demands on their retentive capacity, and they fairly quickly begin to evaluate the second language learning experience and to rate it relative to other areas of the curriculum.

"Attitude" and "motivation" difficult concepts to pin down

It is a commonplace among teachers that a pupil's attitude and motivation in respect of a given subject are crucial. There is undoubtedly a great deal of truth in this proposition; the trouble is, though, that attitude and motivation are extremely nebulous and elastic concepts and it is thus difficult to demonstrate how *precisely* they relate to learning success. With particular regard to second language learning, research undertaken over the last twenty years or so suggests that, whatever else one may say about the nature of this relationship, it is neither uniform for all circumstances nor unidirectional.

Social and psychological distance as factors in L2 acquisition

Language teachers often observe that learners who do well tend to be those who are interested in or favourably disposed towards the culture associated with their target language and the people who speak it. On the other hand, there is plenty of evidence, from both research and everyday experience, that immigrants who feel, or are made to feel, alienated from the life of the community in which they find themselves (Hispanics in the United States, Turks in West Germany, etc.) often fail to acquire more than the most rudimentary command of the language of that community. The obvious inference is that the degree of *social and psychological distance* that exists between a learner and the target language community is of critical importance in relation to the degree of proficiency which that learner will achieve in the language in question.

"Integrative" and "instrumental" orientations in L2 learning

However, other research suggests that life is not quite this simple. One very well known line of investigation in this area begins by drawing a basic distinction between an *integrative* orientation towards the target language community and culture, that is, a positive desire to interact with that community and culture, and an *instrumental* orientation, in other words a utilitarian perspective which sees knowledge of the target language as a means to an end such as further education, employment or a higher salary. Many learners show some measure of both orientations, but mostly one or the other seems to predominate. What is interesting in the present connection, though, is that the effect of the dominance of one or the other orientation seems to vary from learning situation to learning situation. Where the target language is being learned in a context where the associated speech community is relatively easy to make contact with (e.g. French in certain parts of Canada) it appears to be the integrative orientation which is correlated with greater learning success. Where, on the other hand, the target language is being learned essentially as an interna-

14

tional *lingua franca* far from any major population centre of the target language community (e.g. English in the Philippines), success seems to be correlated with instrumental orientation.

Relation between positive motivation and successful learning

To complicate matters further, it is not always entirely clear what the causal relationship is in correlations between attitude/motivation and second language learning success. Some research findings seem to indicate that favourable attitudes towards the target language community actually *develop out of* rather than *underlie* success in learning the second language. If this is so, then clearly language learning success must itself be taken into account as a factor in determining quality of learner motivation. Hence the prevalence of versions of the diagram below in treatments of the role of motivation in second language learning.

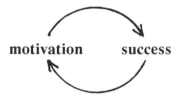

motivation   success

Motivation that arises from the learning situation

If one takes a broad view of language learning success and interprets as success any positive experience which is connected with or results from language learning, one can link the above model to what some commentators have referred to as *internal* sources of motivation, that is, sources of motivation which arise out of the language learning situation as opposed to those which are brought to that situation by the learner. Obvious examples are the general atmosphere in which learning takes place, the degree of relevance of the syllabus, and the interest presented by learning materials and activities.

To summarize, research tends to confirm the widespread intuition that a favourable attitude and a high level of motivation go hand in hand with second language learning success. However, different kinds of

Summary:
favourable
attitude and
high level of
motivation go
hand in hand
with successful
L2 learning

motivation seem to be optimal in different situations, and the nature of the learning experience may itself be a powerful influence in determining attitude and motivation. Authentic texts can fairly obviously have a role in fostering contact with and interest in the culture of the target language and, if sensitively chosen, in making the learning experience enjoyable. With regard to the more "instrumental" dimension, certain kinds of authentic text can be extremely effective in raising learners' consciousness about the career and leisure opportunities that a competence in the language in question makes available.

Suggestions for further reading

A good general introduction to first language acquisition is A. J. Elliot's *Child Language* (Cambridge University Press; 1981). R. Brown's *A First Language* (Cambridge, Mass.: Harvard University Press; 1973) is highly readable but is confined to the acquisition of English.

Two excellent introductions to second language acquisition research are W. T. Littlewood's *Foreign and Second Language Learning* (Cambridge University Press; 1984) and R. Ellis's *Understanding Second Language Acquisition* (Oxford University Press; 1985). The former is quite short and very much oriented towards language teaching issues, whereas the latter gives a fuller account and has a somewhat more theoretical orientation. *Language Two*, by H. Dulay, M. Burt and S. Krashen (New York & London: Oxford University Press; 1982) draws pedagogical conclusions from research findings, especially in those areas with which its authors are particularly associated. *Second Language Acquisition: a Book of Readings*, edited by E. Hatch (Rowley, Mass.: Newbury House; 1978) is a collection of detailed research reports, most of them dealing with the acquisiton of English. H. Wode's *Learning a Second Language 1. An Integrated View of*

Language Acquisition (Tübingen: Gunter Narr; 1981) combines an excellent discussion of theoretical issues with a fascinating account of his own children's acquisition of English.

D. Singleton's article "The fall and rise of language transfer" (in *The Advanced Language Learner*, ed. J. A. Coleman & R. Towell; London: CILT; 1988) surveys the successive phases of research into the influence of the mother tongue on second language learning. For a more complete review of relevant research see H. Ringbom's *The Role of the First Language in Foreign Language Learning* (Clevedon: Multilingual Matters; 1987).

A very useful introduction to the role of attitude and motivation in second language learning is provided by the chapter on motivation in S. McDonough's *Psychology in Foreign Language Teaching* (London: Allen & Unwin; 1981). For a more detailed account see R. Gardner's *Social Psychology and Second Language Learning: the Role of Attitudes and Motivation* (London: Arnold; 1985).

Chapter 2

The communicative approach and authentic texts

Purpose of this chapter

The purpose of this chapter is to summarize the principles that underpin the communicative approach in general and the use of authentic texts as a main source of target language input in particular. Although the communicative approach did not arise directly from language acquisition research, we shall see that in its fundamentals it coincides closely with the findings of that research. We shall also see that the increasingly central role that authentic texts have come to occupy in communicative language teaching methodology can be justified as much in terms of language acquisition research findings as in terms of basic communicative principles.

2.1 Communicative principles

Determining characteristics of the communicative approach

The communicative approach to language teaching derives its name and its essential character from the fact that at every stage - the setting of learning targets, the definition of a syllabus, the development of learning materials, the elaboration and implementation of classroom activities, and the assessment of learners' progress - it focuses on language as a medium of communication. In this it differs from the traditions in language pedagogy that it seeks to replace. Both the grammar-translation and the audio-lingual/audio-visual methods focus from first to last on the grammatical system of the target language; no doubt both methods would claim to be teaching languages for communication, but that is a different matter. The communicative methodologies that have emerged over the past decade and a half have insisted with increasing confidence on the importance of engaging learners in activities which require them to communicate in the target language. We saw in Chapter 1 that children learn language *as* they communicate. By promoting learning not just *for* but *through* communication the communicative approach aligns itself with one of the basic facts of "naturalistic" language acquisition.

Emphasis on communication as a social activity results in learner-centredness

In its most rigorous form, perhaps best exemplified by the "threshold level" specifications and related documents produced by the Council of Europe's modern languages projects, the communicative approach never loses sight of the fact that all communication takes place in a physical setting and between participants, and has a social purpose. The typical communicative syllabus begins by considering who its learners are in terms of such characteristics as age, educational background and previous language learning experience. It then goes on to define the needs that the learners will satisfy by learning the target language, including the communicative purposes that competence in the language will enable them to fulfil. This makes it possible to describe in some detail the kinds of language behaviour that successful learners should be capable of at the end of their course of learning. Thus the learner-centredness of the communicative approach arises directly from an analysis of the social functions of language.

Two common misconceptions corrected

Probably the two most widespread misconceptions about the communicative approach are (i) that it is concerned exclusively with the spoken language, and (ii) that it is indifferent to grammar. The first misconception probably arose because the earliest communicative projects were concerned with learners whose principal need was for a basic competence in oral communication. The Council of Europe's "threshold level" specifications were originally designed to fulfil

Communicative approach not concerned exclusively with spoken language

the needs of migrant workers; and the Graded Objectives movement in the United Kingdom was conceived as a way of bringing foreign language learning within the realistic reach of pupils of lower ability. But it is obvious that in literate societies written language performs a multitude of communicative purposes, so that reading and writing can be as important as listening and speaking in some communicative curricula. (At the same time, because the methods of western education depend so thoroughly on literacy skills, it is easy for teachers to overlook the fact that the great majority of people, including some of the most highly educated, make relatively little use of the writing skill in their daily life once full-time education is behind them.)

Communicative approach not indifferent to grammar

The belief that the communicative approach is indifferent to grammar seems to take two forms. On the one hand there are those who believe that it is hostile to the explicit treatment of grammar as a matter of pedagogical principle. This is not so; indeed, the earliest communicative documents emphasized the need for an eclectic methodology rather than one conforming to any particular orthodoxy. On the other hand there are those who maintain that because the communicative approach is above all interested in exchanges of meaning, it fails to give grammatical form its due. There are two answers to this argument. First, in all languages form and meaning are closely interrelated. It is true that we often succeed in communicating our intended meanings despite formal inadequacies of one kind or another - this frequently happens to all of us not only in foreign languages but also in our first language. However, there is a point beyond which disregard of grammatical form guarantees a breakdown in communication. In a very real sense communication depends on grammar. Secondly, although much communicative methodology gives meaning priority over form, this merely emphasizes the importance of exploring formal issues within a meaningful context; it does not amount to a disregard of grammar. On the contrary, because meaning and form are closely interrelated, the communicative purpose is to discover means of enabling learners to understand more acutely how the forms of their target language are organized in the creation of meaning.

2.2 Authenticity and authentic texts

Authenticity and the need to build bridges into the real world of communication

From the beginning "authenticity" has been one of the key concepts of the communicative movement in language teaching. After all, if we are primarily concerned with language as a medium of communication, we shall want to ensure that there is a strong thread of continuity between what goes on in our classrooms and the characteristic modes of communication in our target language community. One of the most damaging criticisms that can be levelled against language pedagogies that focus on the target language system is that they all too easily leave the learner without secure bridges into the actual world of language use. If its claims are to have any validity, the communicative approach must foster actual communication through the target language in the classroom; for only then can we be sure that our learners are able to communicate through the language. Again we are forcibly reminded of the fact that "naturalistic" language acquisition occurs *through* communication.

Authenticity in four dimensions

Any course of learning involves four obligatory factors: a learner, a goal, content, and a process. The communicative approach is concerned to observe the principle of authenticity in regard to each of them. In other words, it is concerned that in every dimension the course of learning should be appropriate to the learner's needs, expectations and experience on the one hand and to the realities of communication in the target language community on the other.

"Authentic text" defined

Essentially an authentic text is a text that was created to fulfil some social purpose in the language community in which it was produced. Thus novels, poems, newspaper and magazine articles, handbooks and manuals, recipes, and telephone directories are all examples of authentic texts; and so too are radio and television broadcasts and computer programmes. As far as language teaching is concerned, however, "authentic text" has come to have a rather more limited meaning than this. Many attempts to implement the communicative approach have found no use for literary texts (sometimes this is entirely appropriate to the learners' needs, but often it reflects a prejudice against the study of literary texts as a hangover from the grammar-translation method); and even in the last quarter of the twentieth century the physical reality of most classrooms prohibits the frequent use of video or computer materials. Accordingly, when language teachers use the term "authentic text" they often mean a piece of writing that originally appeared in a newspaper or magazine and is probably of ephemeral value and interest. Most language course books published in the past decade have contained their share of authentic texts in this sense of the term. The problem is, of course, that such texts are mostly out of date before the course book is published - which was the reason why *Authentik* had to be invented in the first place.

Why authentic texts should occupy a central role in L2 learning

There are essentially two reasons why authentic texts should occupy a central role in any second language learning process. First, because they have been written for a communicative purpose they are more interesting than texts which have been invented to illustrate the usage of some feature of the target language; learners are thus likely to find them more motivating than invented texts. Secondly, because they revolve around content rather than form, authentic texts are more likely to have acquisition-promoting content than invented texts. Furthermore, it is clear that the child learning its first language or the adult immersed in a second language community enjoys an infinitely higher level of exposure to the target language than a language classroom at some distance from the target language community can easily provide. The teacher can begin to replicate the conditions of "naturalistic" acquisition by using the target language as the normal medium of classroom management and instruction. But a large and varied diet of authentic texts is essential if he or she is to create a genuinely acquisition-rich environment. In the foreign language classroom authentic texts are a substitute for the community of native speakers within which "naturalistic" language acquisition occurs; the more authentic texts we confront our learners with, the more opportunities we shall create for acquisition to take place. Once again the findings of language acquisition research support commonsense intuitions.

"Vertical" and "horizontal" structures: authentic texts as facilitators of natural acquisition processes

We noted in Chapter 1 that children typically acquire the forms of their mother tongue *after* they have learned how to participate in highly organized interaction. They first master the "vertical" structures of discourse, and this provides them with the framework within which they master the "horizontal" structures of syntax and morphology. Thus they acquire language in the very process of using it as a more or less efficient medium of communication: mastery of "horizontal" structures arises from constant practice in the communication of meaning within "vertical" structures. Authentic texts allow the second language learner to follow a parallel course of development.

The knowledge required for comprehension

The precondition for communication, and thus for efficient language acquisition, is comprehension; and comprehension requires access to three kinds of knowledge. First, we need to be able to draw on knowledge of the world, the ever increasing stock of facts and hypotheses that we accumulate from the business of attentive living. This enables us to fix our general bearings and provides us with what might be described as a "plausibility filter": the meanings that we attach to utterances and texts do not conflict with our world knowledge. Secondly, we need to be able to draw on knowledge of the norms of discourse. This knowledge tells us what kind of communicative event we are involved in and helps us to generate appropriate expectations of its structure and outcome. Thirdly, we need to be able to draw on our gradually developing linguistic knowledge, that is, our knowledge of the grammar of the language in question.

It is often assumed that authentic texts are more

Comprehension and authentic texts

difficult for language learners to cope with than invented texts. If coping is a matter of word-for-word translation, this may well be the case. But the comprehension on which effective language acquisition depends is not a matter of word-for-word translation - the child learning its first language cannot, after all, use translation as an aid to learning. It is our contention that if they are properly handled, authentic texts can promote acquisition because they can challenge learners to activate relevant knowledge of the world, of discourse, and of the language system, and thus construct the conditions for further learning. The essential point is that the texts reprinted in *Authentik* belong to types and deal with topics with which learners are already more or less familiar. Clearly, we shall need to provide our learners with various aids to comprehension. But the learners will themselves be able to contribute much in the way of understanding by drawing on their existing knowledge.

Using authentic texts authentically

What we have said so far about authentic texts in relation to language acquisition processes reaffirms the communicative principle that meaning has priority over form. The argument of the preceding paragraphs assumes that authentic texts should be used authentically: that their exploitation in the classroom should be shaped by a general awareness that they were written for a particular communicative purpose. At the same time, we must not overlook the fact that native speakers sometimes focus on form, using their knowledge of the grammar of their mother tongue in order to understand structurally complex passages, or reading authentic texts with a view to enhancing their competence in their mother tongue. In the same way authentic texts provide a living context for the treatment of grammar for foreign language learners.

2.3 From reception to production

Reduced to its most basic terms, our argument is that authentic texts should constitute the primary source of input in any course of language learning because in the classroom only authentic texts can create a sufficiently acquisition-rich environment. Our concern in the remainder of this book is with the question: how do we help our learners to turn *input* into *intake*? In most examinations and many course books, authentic texts serve as little more than comprehension passages. Indeed, one of the few complaints we have received about *Authentik* came from a teacher who apparently wanted to use it as a quarry for comprehension tests and found that we did not provide enough comprehension questions. But if there is any substance in the claims we have made above, work on authentic texts must be capable of going beyond reception to production.

Converting "input" into "intake"

Traditional approaches to the teaching of productive skills in a foreign language start with the forms of words, then move on to syntax at sentence level, and finally combine sentences in discourse. This building-blocks approach makes an undeniable appeal to common sense. However, the model of language acquisition that we have presented in Chapter 1 and appealed to throughout this chapter implies a model of comprehension that moves in the opposite direction, using world and discourse knowledge to establish a framework within which linguistic knowledge can be developed.

Traditional approaches to the teaching of productive skills

For the sake of clarity it is necessary to say something here about words. By suggesting that activities designed to promote productive skills should take discourse as their starting point, we do not mean to imply that words somehow come last in the productive process. At all levels of linguistic reflection and analysis nothing can be achieved without words. We recall much of our world knowledge and refer to all of it in words; and the structure of any discourse depends crucially on the words we use. It is not words themselves that should be our final concern in the productive process, however,

Words and their role in the productive process

but the way in which they relate to one another. We also do not mean to imply that the productive process is a straightforward matter of moving downwards through a hierarchy of functions. Constructing an appropriate piece of discourse involves planning, production and monitoring on various levels, and we move up and down these with great flexibility.

A look ahead to Chapter 3

Chapter 3 examines some of the activities and exercise types that have been used with authentic texts and begins to suggest how the model of language learning we have presented in this and the previous chapter can be implemented. In particular we seek to show how learners can exploit the knowledge that they bring to the learning task. We assume that they are capable of much more creative work than is often supposed, always provided they are given time and space in which to learn. Finally, the activities and

Towards learner autonomy

exercise types we recommend are capable of fostering a high degree of learner autonomy. We attach great importance to this, for logically only those who achieve a significant level of autonomy as language learners are likely to have the confidence to remain adventurous and efficient language users through their adult life.

Suggestions for further reading

The most important of the Council of Europe's communicative language syllabuses are *The Threshold Level* by J. van Ek (Strasbourg; 1975), *Un Niveau Seuil* by D. Coste, J. Courtillon, V. Ferenczi, M. Martins-Baltar & E. Papo (Strasbourg; 1976), and *Kontaktschwelle* by M. Baldegger, M. Müller, G. Schneider & A. Näf (Strasbourg; 1980). *Graded Objectives in Modern Languages*, by A. Harding, B. Page & S. Rowell (London: CILT; 1980) provides a useful overview of early attempts to implement a communicative approach in British schools. For an up-to-date account of the evolution of communicative syllabus design see D.

Nunan's *Syllabus Design* (Oxford University Press; 1988).

H. G. Widdowson's *Teaching Language as Communication* (Oxford University Press; 1978) is one of the most durable contributions to the debate on communicative language teaching. Its concern with language as discourse means that it contains a wealth of material relevant to the use of authentic texts in second language teaching. The same concern characterizes most of the articles and papers in Widdowson's two collections, *Explorations in Applied Linguistics I* and *Explorations in Applied Linguistics II* (Oxford University Press; 1979 & 1984).

Interactive Language Teaching, edited by W. M. Rivers (Cambridge University Press; 1987), reflects the growing concern of methodologists to provide for as much interaction as possible, not only between learners as they use their target language to communicate with one another but also between the individual learner and the target language.

Chapter 3

Exercise types for use with authentic texts

Purpose of this chapter

This chapter discusses and illustrates some of the exercises and activities that can be used to bring learners into sustained interaction with authentic texts. Our textual examples and many of the exercises attached to them are taken from issues of *Authentik* published in 1987-8. It should be noted, however, that because many of our examples originally formed part of exercise chains, they may have had a somewhat different purpose from the one described in our analysis. We have included examples in three languages partly to underline the fact that French, German and Spanish exist in the curriculum by equal right, but partly also in order to give most readers the opportunity to work through some exercises without the benefit of fluency, as though they were learners themselves. Although for reasons of economy our discussion is confined to printed texts, many of the activities we shall mention can also be used, with or without adaptation, with audio texts.

Structure and content of this chapter

We begin the chapter with a summary of our general principles, which follow directly from Chapters 1 and 2; then we look at the forms of comprehension exercise that have traditionally been used with authentic texts and consider their limitations as well as their usefulness; we go on to outline an approach to comprehension based on productive activities that are designed to overcome these limitations; next we consider how to use authentic texts as a basis for productive exercises; after that we suggest ways of using authentic texts to teach grammar and vocabulary; and we conclude the chapter by discussing the use of authentic texts in relation to some of the practical and organizational constraints that all teachers have to contend with.

3.1 General principles

The general principles that determine how we seek to exploit authentic texts should be firmly based on the aims that our language teaching is calculated to fulfil. These have one general and two more specific dimensions. First, there is the aim of the foreign language curriculum as laid down in the Department of Education's *Rules and Programme*, which is to give the learner a communicative competence in the target language corresponding to his or her needs, expectations and interests. This aim reminds us (as we saw in Chapter 2) that communication is a social activity, but also that the learner is an individual. Secondly, there is a special version of this aim that arises from our use of authentic texts: the aim to enable the learner to develop, as part of his or her communicative competence, the capacity to make an authentic response to authentic texts; that is, a response to texts as communicative events and not just examples of the target language. Thirdly, since authentic texts will in principle be available to them long after they have left school, we should have the aim of helping our learners to learn for life. In other words, we should want them to become confident that at any time in the future they can pick up a newspaper or magazine in French, German or Spanish and make something of it. This means that work on authentic texts should be explicitly concerned to develop learners' autonomy.

In deciding how best to fulfil these aims we need a model of the language learning process. In Chapter 1 we saw how all "naturalistic" language acquisition takes place *through* interaction and *through* communication, and in Chapter 2 we argued that communicative language teaching is essentially defined in these terms. In Chapter 2 we also argued that a large part of the rationale for using authentic texts as a central component of language teaching resides in the capacity of such

The aims of language teaching

Communicative competence and authentic texts

Learning for life

A model of the language learning process

texts to create an acquisition-rich environment in which learners can interact not only with one another but also with the target language. It is important to stress this latter form of interaction. Most methodological proposals for communicative language teaching assign a central role to group and pair work as a means of creating the conditions for communication in the classroom. This reflects the fact that all linguistic communication is in some sense social activity, and it provides for the possibility of learning *through* communication. However, we must not overlook the fact that social interaction is not all that is involved in successful language learning. All learners, whether they are children learning their first language or adolescents or adults learning a foreign language, need time and space in which to integrate the new material that they learn with what they already know. No doubt the process of integration can begin during social interaction, but its successful completion requires that learners spend time on their own (sometimes when they are in the presence of others).

Group and pair work in the communicative approach

Learning as an individual process

Methodological implications of the model

This model of the language learning process implies the following general methodological principles:

(i) As far as possible the target language should be the language of classroom management and instruction. This may seem a hopeless aspiration to those who habitually teach foreign languages through English; but the fact is that teaching through the medium of the target language requires a relatively limited repertoire on the part of the teacher and a very limited repertoire on the part of the learner. This principle should also extend to written instructions for exercises and activities, though it is not always complied with in the examples that follow.

(ii) Many of the exercises and activities used should require learners to communicate with one another through the target language, which implies a large measure of group and pair work.

(iii) Some exercises and activities should be designed explicitly to help learners integrate new material with what they already know. This implies a recognition that essential parts of the learning process are solitary (some of them of course work below the level of consciousness). It is important to note that learners can be on their own while remaining in the physical presence of thirty other learners.

3.2 Focus on comprehension

(i) Traditional approaches

Comprehension questions
Our first four examples are of traditional types of comprehension exercise, using multiple-choice or open questions in English or the target language. These are also the means used to test comprehension of written texts in public examinations. It is worth working through these four examples carefully (however little Spanish or German one may know), trying to capture the techniques one uses in arriving at an answer.

EXAMPLE 1

ABC Jueves,
31.12.87

Encuentran lleno de cerdos un turismo robado en Orense

Orense, **Efe**

Un turismo Seat 850, que le había sido sustraído al vecino de San Ciprián de Viñas E.B.M., fue recuperado horas después por la Policía en la avenida de Zamora, cargado con cerdos de tres y cuatro meses.

Según la denuncia formulada en Comisaría, el propietario había dejado estacionado su vehículo en las immediaciones de su domicilio, de donde desapareció en el curso de la mañana del martes.

Efectivos policiales localizaron el vehículo horas después, en la capital de la provincia y con media docena de cerdos que ocupaban la parte posterior del turismo, alguno de ellos sobre los propios asientos.

El turismo tenía hecho el puente en el sistema de encendido y, por estar bastante deteriorado, su propietario no lo había valorado en más de cinco mil pesetas. Una vez recuperado, el ganado fue trasladado por la Policía al recinto en el que se celebra la feria de ganado.

Mult - choice
Open questions
in English

Choose the correct answers from the following:
1. (a) the car was stolen with 3 or 4 pigs in it
   (b) the car was empty when stolen
   (c) there were some pigs in the car when it was stolen
2. (a) the owner parked the car near his home
   (b) he left the car near the police station
   (c) the car was stolen immediately after it was parked
3. (a) half a dozen policemen found the car
   (b) a tourist was also in the back of the car
   (c) there were pigs in the back of the car
4. (a) the car was worth much more than 5,000 pesetas
   (b) the car was started without a key (hot-wired)
   (c) a party was held to celebrate the recovery of the pigs

EXAMPLE 2

Ya, 9.3.88

Apuñalaron a un cliente
Cuatro niños atracan un banco en Valencia

Valencia/E.P.

Cuatro niños de edades comprendidas entre 12 y 16 años atracaron en la mañana del lunes una sucursal de la Caja de Ahorros de Valencia. Los menores irrumpieron en el banco armados con varias navajas, con las que amenazaron a los empleados y clientes. Tras apoderarse de ciento veinte mil pesetas, un cliente les hizo frentes, siendo agredido con una navaja por uno de los menores, que le provocó heridas de gravedad.

Cuando los asaltantes intentaban escapar, los empleados de la sucursal bancaria bloquearon las puertas del local y consiguieron que uno de los niños quedara retenido entre las puertas de entrada y de salida, donde fue detenido poco después, al igual que los otros tres menores, que fueron capturados en las inmediaciones de la sucursal.

Multiple-choice
questions in
target language

Choose the correct answer for each of the following:
1. Los jóvenes atracaron el banco
   (a) entre mediodía y las cuatro de la tarde
   (b) armados con navajas
   (c) amenazando a los empleados con una escopeta
   (d) sin violencia
2. Uno de los niños
   (a) hizo frente a un empleado
   (b) se sentó cerca de la puerta de entrada
   (c) asaltó al cliente que no quería seguir sus órdenes

        (d)   se cayó
3. Los empleados de banco
        (a)   bloquearon las puertas de la sucursal
        (b)   intentaron escapar
        (c)   asaltaron a los atracadores
        (d)   escaparon a la calle
4. Robaron
        (a)   12.000 ptas.
        (b)   20.000 ptas.
        (c)   200.000 ptas.
        (d)   120.000 ptas.
5. Después capturaron
        (a)   a tres heridos
        (b)   a uno de los niños
        (c)   a los cuatro atracadores
        (d)   a tres niños de la localidad

EXAMPLE 3

Neue Post,
24.7.87

Skandalöser Giftgas-Unfall brachte Altenheim-bewohner in tödliche Gefahr
Weil ein Angestellter schlampte, wurden 13 pflege-bedürftige Frauen und Männer Opfer des Unglücks
"Es war schrecklich", erinnert sich die 71jährige Adelheid Stury, Bewohnerin des Münchner Hans-Sieber-Altenheims. "Ich habe kaum noch Luft bekommen können und glaubte, jeden Moment elend ersticken zu müssen."

Auch ihre Zimmernachbarin Julia Denk (81) überkommt heute noch Angst, wenn sie an jenes Ereignis zurückdenkt, das sie fast das Leben gekostet hätte. "Todesangst habe ich gehabt", sagt die alte Dame. "Eine Angst, wie ich sie meinem ärgsten Feind nicht wünsche."

An einem Montag war es passiert. Karl Mayerhofer, Leiter der Bade- und Therapie-Abteilung des Senioren-heims, in dem rund 300 alte Menschen leben, hatte gerade eine Patientin im Sitzstuhl ins Schwimmbecken gelassen, als er einen übel stechenden Gasgeruch bemerkte.

"Ich wusste sofort, dass es sich um Chlorgas handelte", erzählt der 42jährige Bademeister. Keuchend lief Karl Mayer-hofer in die Anmeldung der Badeabteilung und alarmierte sofort Heimleiter Bertram Gruber. Der rief Polizei und Feuerwehr an und trommelte über Funk sämtliche Mitarbeiter zusammen.

"Wir hatten gerade zu Mittag gegessen", erinnert er sich. "Einige unserer alten Leute machten ihren Mittagsschlaf. Ausserdem haben wir natürlich auch einige Pflegefälle im Heim. Unvorstellbar, was passiert wäre, wenn sich das Gas durch alle Räume ausgebreitet hätte."

Umgehend liess Bertram Gruber die bettlägerigen Pa-

33

tienten evakuieren. Diejenigen Senioren, die sich zum Mittagsschlaf hingelegt hatten, wurden geweckt und in Sicherheit gebracht - einige konnten alleine gehen, andere wurden in Rollstühle gesetzt oder mit ihren Betten ins Freie geschoben.

Einer der Bewohner berichtet: "Nur der Geistesgegenwart von Herrn Mayerhofer und Herrn Gruber sowie dem Einsatz der übrigen Helfer ist zu verdanken, dass es nicht zu einer grossen Katastrophe kam."

Dennoch: 13 pflegebedürftige Frauen und Männer mussten mit zum Teil schweren Chlorgasvergiftungen ins Krankenhaus eingeliefert werden. Bleibende Schäden aber befürchten die Ärzte bei keinem von ihnen.

Ausgelöst wurde der skandalöse Giftgasunfall durch die Schlamperei eines 47jährigen Heizungsarbeiters. "Obwohl im Heizungsraum grosse Hinweisschilder vor der Gefahr warnen", sagt Bademeister Mayerhofer, "hat er einfach Salzsäure in die Reinigungsmaschinen des Schwimmbekkens gefüllt. Sofort bildete sich hochgiftiges Chlorgas, das über Liftschächte ins ganze Haus zog."

Open questions in English

Answer the following questions:
1. Who was the first to notice that there was something wrong?
2. What attracted his attention?
3. What was he doing at the time?
4. What was his immediate reaction?
5. What did the director of the old folks' home do?
6. At what time of day did the accident happen?
7. How did the personnel and other helpers evacuate the old people? What did they have to do first?
8. How many people needed hospital treatment?
9. Who caused the accident? Where did the poisonous gas come from?
10. How did it seep into the building?

EXAMPLE 4

Basler Zeitung,
24.12.86

Des Weihnachtsmannes Domizil

Der Weihnachtsmann, der ja schon eine Wohnung beispielsweise in North Pole in Alaska und an einigen anderen Orten auf der Welt hat, besitzt auch in Finnland ein festes Domizil. Von den Fremdenverkehrsbehörden ist ihm dieses zwar nicht am Nordpol, aber doch nahe am Polarkreis, in Rovaniemi, zugewiesen worden, rund 2500 Kilometer vom nördlichsten Punkt der Erde entfernt. Und ausgestattet ist dieses Domizil mit Werkstätte und einer Kurzwellenradiostation, alles in der Hoffnung, dass dies

Touristen aus aller Welt in den hohen Norden Finnlands locken könne. Um für sich selbst und für Finnland zu werben ist der finnische Nikolaus schon weit gereist, nach Los Angeles und Singapur beispielsweise. Und aus der Schweiz hat er schon 20, aus Beverly Hills in Kalifornien 50 Kinder nach Rovaniemi geholt, damit sie sich seinen Wohnsitz mit eigenen Augen anschauen konnten.

Sein «Reich» ist ein rund 112 000 Quadratkilometer grosses Stück arktischer Wildnis, in dem neben mehr als 300 000 Rentieren auch knapp 200 000 Menschen leben. Die amtliche Adresse des Weihnachtsmannes lautet: 99999 Korvatunturi, Finnland. Er selbst oder einer seiner Helfer werde jeden Brief beantworten, der einen Absender trage, wird versichert. Ein internationales Unternehmen hat ihm einen Computer gestiftet, damit er es leichter hat, die rund 200 000 Briefe zu beantworten, die ihm dieses Jahr Kinder aus 90 Ländern geschrieben haben. Amateurfunker können den Weihnachtsmann angeblich unter dem Rufzeichen OH9SCL erreichen.

Open questions in target language

Lies den Artikel und beantworte die folgenden Fragen:
1. Wo wohnt der finnische Weihnachtsmann?
2. Wie weit ist seine Wohnung vom Nordpol entfernt?
3. Wie gross ist sein Reich? Wieviele Menschen wohnen dort?
4. Wie lautet die Adresse?
5. Wieviele Briefe hat der Weihnachtsmann im letzten Jahr bekommen? Aus wievielen verschiedenen Ländern?
6. Wie kann man den Weihnachtsmann auch noch erreichen, per Funk oder per Telefon? Wie lautet die Nummer?

Examples 1-4 discussed

In the sense that it does not require the learner to formulate an answer, whether in English or the target language, the multiple-choice format used in Examples 1 and 2 is clearly easier to deal with than the open-question format used in Examples 3 and 4. Example 1 draws attention to the fact that in devising multiple-choice questions it is not always easy to find plausible alternatives. However, although this is a serious matter in an examination or test, it is much less serious in an exercise designed for use in the clasroom.

How is the difficulty of the task affected by the language in which the questions are couched? Questions in English require the learner to be able in some sense to translate from English to the target language and back again; and they are likely to offer him very little help in unlocking those parts of the target language text that are opaque to him. Questions in the target language, on the other hand, may actually help the learner to understand the text better; though they may also encourage him to tackle the task by a process of word-identification that involves a minimum of comprehension. This is especially true of the multiple-choice format. Open questions in the target language require not only comprehension but production, and in some cases may presuppose a relatively sophisticated competence in the target language; in other words, Example 4 is potentially a much more difficult task to accomplish well than Examples 1-3.

Comprehension questions and "comprehension frame"

In principle comprehension questions can provide the learner with a "comprehension frame", that is, a preliminary outline of the thematic structure of the text - the more questions there are, the more likely they are to benefit the learner in this way. Thus work on the questions *before* the text is read can do much to facilitate comprehension. However, the other side of this coin is that the questions inevitably impose one particular focus on the text and thus inevitably limit the learner's approach to it.

Limitations of traditional approaches to comprehension

Whatever their virtues as test types, exercises of the kind exemplified in Examples 1-4 have no very obvious advantages as promoters of interactive language learning. For one thing they encourage a limited approach to the authentic text and ensure that much will be left out of account; for another they have only limited usefulness as the focus for group or pair work - two heads may well be better than one, but the nature of the activity is not guaranteed to promote the negotiation of meaning in the target language which is the basis of communicative learning. What is more, exercises of this kind take quite a lot of time and effort to devise, which is appropriate to a question on a public examination paper but not necessarily to a learning activity that will occupy a class for perhaps half a lesson.

A variant on the traditional approach

Example 5 offers an interesting variant on the traditional comprehension exercise: if these are the answers, what are the questions?

EXAMPLE 5

El Independiente,
5.12.87

Seat entrega Málaga 100.000

Seat ha fabricado y vendido ya más de cien mil unidades de su modelo Málaga, que tan buena acogida tiene tanto en el mercado español como en los mercados exteriores.

El fabricante hispano que exporta en estos momentos a treinta países tiene previsto cerrar el presente ejercicio con más de 155.000 millones de pesetas de facturación en concepto de ventas al exterior.

The answers are given: the learner has to work out what the questions were

Here is a comprehension exercise with a difference. Instead of having to answer questions, you are given the answers and have to supply appropriate questions.

1. ¿..?
                Una compañía que fabrica automóviles.
2. ¿..?
                Cien mil.
3. ¿..?
                Sí, tanto en España como en el extranjero.
4. ¿..?
                Treinta países.
5. ¿..?
                155.000 millones de pesetas.

Example 5 discussed

Although it requires the same level of competence in the target language as Example 4, Example 5 may by its very unusualness involve the learner in a less constrained interaction with the target language text than a traditional comprehension exercise. And its reversal of expected procedures begins to suggest a means of exploiting traditional comprehension exercises in a manner more likely to involve learners in interaction both with one another and with the target language. We made the point above that devising exercises of this kind is a time-consuming activity; but the time will be well spent if it is the learners who devise the exercise. It is

Getting learners to devise their own exercises

possible to envisage an activity that begins by asking individual learners to devise five comprehension questions for homework; continues by putting learners in groups to construct a finished exercise; and ends by having the groups exchange and compare exercises.

(ii) Comprehension by evaluation of content

More indirect approaches to comprehension

Concern that traditional approaches to teaching comprehension were insufficiently interactive was doubtless one of the considerations that led to the development of exercise types that approach comprehension rather more indirectly. Our next three examples all require the learner to evaluate the content of the text in one way or another. In Example 6 the learner has to decide whether a number of statements about Madonna are true or false; in Example 7 he has to decide which elements of the report about Charlie Nicholas are positive and which negative; and in Example 8 he has to extract from the text two lists of words and phrases, one concerned with victory and the other concerned with defeat.

EXAMPLE 6

Podium Hit,
9.87

La nouvelle Madonna

Seuls les beatles étaient arrivés à un tel résultat, dans les années soixante, mais Madonna a pulvérisé leur record. Une sacrée revanche pour la petite inconnue arrivée à New York en 1978 avec quelques dollars en poche, depuis son Michigan natal, et qui peut se vanter, à présent, d'être la seule chanteuse à avoir été cinq fois numéro un des ventes aux Etats-Unis au cours des cinq dernières années. En ce moment, Madonna, longtemps dénigrée par la presse de son pays, fait la une de bien des journaux. Elle a eu droit à la couverture de *Cosmopolitan*, et pour la première fois depuis un bon bout de temps, elle s'est confiée à plusieurs journalistes. Il faut dire qu'elle n'est pas très disponible, vu le planning imposé par le tour qui l'a entraînée des Etats-Unis jusqu'au Japon, en attendant l'Europe. Partout, le public a été frappé par sa transformation physique. Ella a perdu plusieurs kilos et arbore une ligne absolument superbe. Cette métamorphose, elle la doit à un changement radical d'alimentation. Madonna est végétarienne, et elle se contente, par exemple, à l'heure du déjeuner, d'un verre de lait de soja, d'une pomme et de chips de riz.

En ce moment, on parle encore de divorce entre Madonna et Sean Penn. L'intéressée est muette sur le sujet. On ne peut savoir ce qui sera passé entre le moment où cet article a été écrit et sa publication, mais une chose est certaine: les Penn ont chacun une personnalité explosive, et il est normal qu'il y ait souvent des étincelles entre eux. Cela dit, quand Madonna parle de celui pour qui elle eut le coup de foudre, dès leur première rencontre, elle dit des choses très tendres. Vous voulez une preuve? Madonna a horreur des chiens. Elle ne les supporte pas. En revanche, Sean les adore. Pendant le tournage du nouveau film de Madonna, «Who's that girl», le coiffeur de Griffin Dunne, le partenaire de Madonna, est arrivé un jour sur le plateau avec la photo de sa chienne et des petits qu'elle venait d'avoir. Qu'a fait Madonna? Elle est allée chercher l'un des chiots puis elle est rentrée jusqu'à sa villa. Là, elle a laissé l'animal devant la porte, puis elle a dit négligemment à Sean, qui était dans la maison: «Tu devrais aller dehors. Il y a quelqu'un qui voudrait faire ta connaissance». Quand Sean Penn a vu qui l'attendait, Madonna dit que son mari a été à deux doigts de se mettre à pleurer. Et après ça on dira que ces deux-là ne s'aiment pas! A d'autres... D'autant plus que cette adoption représentait pour Madonna un véritable sacrifice. Elle ne regrette rien, car Sean est fou de son chien. «Et en plus, avoue Madonna en riant, j'ai choisi un de ces chiens qui deviennent aussi grands et costauds qu'un ours! Moi qui ne voulait pas d'un animal qui perd des poils sur les coussins...» Elle sait être vraiment touchante, Madonna. Ses problèmes avec son père, elle a aussi fini par les résoudre. Depuis l'enfance, elle lui en voulait, à ce père qui n'avait attendu que deux ans pour se remarier, alors que sa première femme - la mère de Madonna - était morte d'un cancer. Madonna n'avait que six ans quand elle perdit sa mère. «Je crois que c'est ce chagrin qui m'a donné l'envie de devenir quelqu'un, de me battre.» C'est aussi pourquoi elle a voulu régler ses comptes avec ce père qui ne la comprenait pas, lorsqu'elle chanta «Papa don't preach».

Il ne reste plus à Madonna qu'à faire la conquête de Paris, et le monde entier sera à ses pieds.

Robert de Laroche

Lisez l'article sur Madonna et marquez VRAI ou FAUX pour chaque phrase.

1. Madonna vient d'ajouter un nouveau disque à son palmarès.

Ten statements, some true and some false, to be evaluated on the basis of the authentic text

2. A son arrivée à New York en 1978, Madonna était bien connue du public.
3. Elle a décidé de parler à la presse pour la première fois depuis longtemps.
4. Madonna a maigri grâce à un changement de régime.
5. Madonna parle beaucoup des bruits qui courent sur son divorce possible d'avec son mari Sean Penn.
6. Madonna aime bien les gros chiens.
7. Madonna a fait cadeau d'un tout petit chien à Sean Penn.
8. Sean Penn a été vraiment touché.
9. Madonna ne s'entend toujours pas avec son père.
10. Madonna était très heureuse avec son père dans son enfance.

EXAMPLE 7

L'Equipe,
26-27.9.87

Très cher Nicholas!
Après Hoddle et Hateley, un troisième britannique sur la Côte?

Placé sur la liste des transferts par Arsenal, Charlie Nicholas a déclaré qu'il souhaitait venir tenter sa chance en France: «Depuis que j'ai découvert le football français lors des deux dernières Coupes du monde je pense sincèrement que mon style de jeu est taillé sur mesure pour la France.»

Toulon qui est à la recherche d'un attaquant s'est aussitôt intéressé à l'Ecossais. C'est ce que nous a confirmé Rolland Courbis, l'entraîneur des Varois: «Nicholas fait effectivement partie des trois ou quatre joueurs avec qui nous sommes en contact. Tous appartiennent à la CEE. Aucune décision ne sera prise avant le 8 octobre au lendemain de Toulon-Laval (1).»

Nicholas a été écarté de l'équipe pro par George Graham l'entraîneur des «Gunners» pour insuffisance de performances et est proposé «à la vente» pour 6 millions de francs. Un somme qui fait tiquer le SC Toulonet Rolland Courbis!

Nicholas était arrivé à Arsenal voilà quatre ans. Le club londonien avait dû débourser 7,5 millions de francs pour obtenir sa signature. Le Celtic de Glasgow auquel appartenait Charlie est aujourd'hui disposé à le récupérer, mais préfère attendre, espérant qu'Arsenal sera contraint de baisser ses prétentions.

Nicholas qui vient de signer pour quatre années supplémentaires avec Arsenal évolue désormais avec l'équipe réserve. Où, paraît-il, ses prestations sont d'une rare médiocrité. Inutile de préciser que du côté des

dirigeants londoniens on regrette amèrement d'avoir pro-
longé le contrat de l'Ecossais. Mais on se souvient qu'en fin
de saison dernière il avait permis aux Gunners de remporter
la Littlewood's Cup en marquant un but et en réussissant
une passe décisive.

Soutenu par le public de Highbury qui apprécie son jeu
spectaculaire, Nicholas s'était vu offrir un contrat juteux
puisque son salaire est fixé à 80 000 francs par mois. Ce qui
en Angleterre est exceptionnel! Reste à savoir si l'Ecossais
qui évolue plutôt milieu offensif qu'attaquant de pointe est le
joueur qui correspond à ce que recherche le S-G Toulon!
C.B.

(1) Courbis nous a confirmé qu'il n'était pas question que
Bosman devienne Toulonnais cette saison, démentant ainsi
certaines informations indiquant que le Hollandais pourrait
signer à Toulon dès cette semaine.

**Positive and
negative
elements to be
extracted from
authentic text**

Charlie Nicholas est un joueur de football à vendre. L'équipe
de Toulon s'y intéresse. Pouvez-vous les aider à prendre une
décision? Commencez en remplissant les cases ci-dessous.

éléments positifs	éléments négatifs

EXAMPLE 8

L'Equipe,
5.10.87

Le forcené de la Tour
Cet homme exténué dans les escaliers de la tour Eiffel est
un Américain de trente-neuf ans, Steve Silva. Il a tenté en
vain, samedi, de battre ce que le *Livre Guinness des records*
appelle le "mile vertical", c'est à dire sept fois et demi la
hauteur de la tour Eiffel. Pour battre le record, Steve Silva
devait monter et descendre les 1 792 marches de la tour en
2 h 1'34". Il a finalement échoué de quatre-vingt-dix secon-
des.

L'Equipe,
3-4.10.87

Swing champion
Au début du tournoi la foule ne le connaissait que sous
l'appellation du "petit rouquin qui en veut". En trois jours *Ian
Woosnam* prouvait qu'on pouvait ne mesurer que 1,64 m et
être le plus fort. Non seulement le vainqueur du Trophée
Lancôme écrasant tous ces champions immenses, irlan-
dais, écossais, allemands, américains, sud-africains, sans
compter le plus fameux de tous, l'espagnol Ballesteros, mais

désormais classé numéro un européen! Un titre qui lui a rapporté, à Saint-Nom, 500 000 francs, mais qui ne lui suffit pas. C'est numéro un mondial qu'il veut désormais être. Et dire qu'il y a quelques années à peine, le Gallois hésitait entre la petite balle et le ballon rond ...

Specific elements to be extracted from authentic texts

Lisez les deux textes. Faites un liste des éléments linguistiques qui illustrent la victoire et de ceux qui illustrent la défaite.

Discussion of Examples 6-8

Like the more traditional comprehension exercises, Example 6 belongs to a kind that learners could well devise themselves, using the procedures outlined above. Examples 7 and 8 lend themselves less obviously to this treatment, but they have in their favour that they require very little preparation on the part of the teacher. They belong to a class of activity that is easy to devise and organize and can lead to a high level of interaction. For example, one can get the learners to work in groups scanning a single text, a page of texts, or a whole newspaper looking for good news and bad news. The very fact that they are asked to evaluate the content of the authentic text in one way or another involves their affective faculties and is thus calculated to lead them to at least the beginnings of an authentic response to an authentic text.

(iii) Information extraction

Information extraction

Closely related to the activities we have just been considering are those that approach comprehension as a matter of extracting information from the authentic text. Thus Example 9 requires the learner to extract from a text about Christopher Lambert information that might be used in a "wanted" poster:

EXAMPLE 9

Bravo, 5.87

Er flog aus vier Schulen

"Er ist ein Typ, der sein Leben in seine Hände genommen hat. Ein Rebell, der sich gegen die drei Mächte in Sizilien auflehnte: die Kirche, den Adel, die Mafia. Er machte seinen Weg, er kämpfte gegen die Ungerechtigkeiten. Er war einer, der immer die Verantwortung für seine Taten übernahm, und er war auch ein grosser Romantiker, sehr idealistisch."

So beschreibt der 30jährige Christopher Lambert den gefürchtesten, bei den Armen des Landes aber auch verehrtesten Banditen Siziliens, Salvatore Giuliano. Lambert ist Giuliano in dem Action-Streifen "Der Sizilianer".

Christopher, der sich privat sehr lässig kleidet (meist Cordhose und Lederjacke), sucht nach seiner Brille. Er ist extrem kurzsichtig. "In meinen Filmen trage ich Haftschalen."

Christopher (in seiner Wahlheimat Frankreich schreibt er sich übrigens ohne r am Schluss) kam in New York zur Welt. Sein Vater war damals Diplomat bei den Vereinten Nationen und wechselte oft den Wohnort. Als Christopher ein Jahr alt war, zogen seine Eltern mit ihm nach Genf. Dort ging er auch zur Schule.

Christopher: "Ich war ein verdammt zerstreuter Schüler. Hatte nur Streiche im Sinn. Ich bin insgesamt von vier Schulen geflogen. Mein Vater war richtig sauer."

Nach dem Abitur (Christopher: "In den letzten Schuljahren habe ich wie ein Wilder gebüffelt") leistete er in Grenoble seinen Militärdienst bei den Alpenjägern ab. Anschliessend trat er als Praktikant in eine Bank in London ein. Dieser Job war ihm zu langweilig. Er ging nach Paris und wurde am Konservatorium zugelassen.

1980 drehte er seinen ersten Film "Le Bar du Telephone". Drei Jahre später ist er Tarzan in "Greystoke - Die Legende von Tarzan, Herr der Affen". Er wird ein Star. Weitere Filme: "Duett zu dritt", "Subway", "Highlander" und "I love you".

Privat ist Christopher mit der bildhübschen Schauspielerin Diane Lane ("Hautnah") heftig verbandelt.

Write a "wanted" poster based on information contained in the authentic text

Schreiben Sie einen "Steckbrief" für Christopher Lambert:

Name:
Alter:
Geburtsort:
Nationalität
Eltern (Beruf):
Schulbildung:
Militärdienst:
Ausbildung:
Filme:
Besondere Kennzeichen:

There are many possible variants on this approach to comprehension. For example, learners can work indi-

Other types of information-extraction exercise

vidually, in pairs, or in groups, filling out grids that analyse a single text or a whole page of a newspaper in terms of WHO?, WHAT?, WHEN? and WHERE? The same approach can be used to compare two or more reports of the same event or descriptions of the same person or place. Like activities that require an evaluative response from the learner, this kind of activity can lead to highly stimulating interaction; and once again it requires little preparation on the part of the teacher.

A further variant

Example 10 illustrates a rather different kind of activity that depends on extracting information from the authentic text: one newspaper report is used as the basis for re-ordering a jumbled version of another report of the same event.

EXAMPLE 10

En Diario 16, 8.10.87

Veinte heridos
Siete muertos en un accidente de tráfico por colisión de una moto y un autobús

IBIZA. - Una colisión frontal entre una moto de 850 centímetros cúbicos y un autocar con treinta y cinco turistas alemanes produjo ayer siete muertos y 20 heridos en Ibiza.

De los heridos, ocho con graves quemaduras fueron evacuados en helicóptero al hospital de la Fe de Valencia, según informó la Guardia Civil de Tráfico. En este centro sanitario se dispone de una unidad especial para este tipo de heridos. Todos ellos se encuentran en estado muy grave con quemaduras muy importantes.

El accidente se produjo a las 13,30 en el kilómetro 6,500 de la carretera entre Ibiza y Portinatx, en el término municipal de Santa Eulalia del Río.

Al parecer la colisión se produjo cuando la moto, marca *Guzzi*, adelantó a un vehículo y se empotró en el autocar.

Use the above article to put the following pieces of a report of the same event in the right order:

Una colisión frontal entre una moto de 850 centímetros cúbicos y un autocar con turistas alemanes, algunos de los cuales regresaban hoy,

De éstos, ocho permancen graves, con quemaduras de consideración en su cuerpo, en el hospital de La Fe, de Valencia,

Ibiza y Portinatx, comarcal 733, en el término municipal de Santa Eulalia del Río.

provocando el incendio del autobús en el que viajaban treinta y cinco turistas de nacionalidad alemana, seis de los cuales también fallecieron.

adonde fueron evacuados en helicóptero y aviocar, por contar con una unidad especial para este tipo de heridos.

Al parecer, la colisión se produjo cuando la moto Guzzi de gran clindrada adelantó

De resultas de la violenta colisión, el conductor de la moto, al parecer de nacionalidad italiana, resultó muerto en el acto y el depósito de gasolina de la motocicleta estalló,

a un vehículo y se empotró en el autocar.

iban dos ocupantes.

El accidente se produjo a la una y media de la tarde de ayer en el kilómetro 6,500 de la carretera entre

jueves, a su país de origen tras las vacaciones, produjo ayer siete muertos y más de una veintena de heridos.

Noticias no confirmadas indican que en la moto

Once you have put these pieces together, compare the information provided in the two articles under the headings TIME, LOCATION, HOW THE ACCIDENT HAPPENED, NUMBER OF VICTIMS, VEHICLES INVOLVED.

3.3 From production to reception

In Chapter 1 we saw how naturalistic language acquisition continuously exploits the learner's existing knowledge; in particular we saw how what we called

"Naturalistic" acquisition exploits the learner's existing knowledge

"horizontal structures", the morpho-syntactic forms of a language, are acquired within a framework of "vertical structures" established by developing knowledge of the norms of interaction. All learning is a matter of integrating new knowledge with what we already know, and the comprehension exercises we have illustrated in 3.2 all presuppose a fair degree of linguistic knowledge. They are organized in such a way that the learner is unable to exploit his world knowledge unless he possesses a minimum of grammatical, lexical and discourse knowledge; and this means that they have limited potential for language *learning* as opposed to language *practice*. It is difficult to use them successfully in the early stages of learning. If the learner is to begin

Activating the language learner's existing knowledge

to derive from his diet of authentic texts the benefits claimed in Chapters 1 and 2, we must devise ways of activating his world and discourse knowledge while at the same time compensating for deficiencies in his linguistic (grammatical and lexical) knowledge.

(i) Predictive activities

One way of activating the learner's world and discourse knowledge is to involve him in predictive activities of the kind illustrated in Example 11.

EXAMPLE 11

Preparatory task: put nine sentences in a plausible chronological order and edit them into a coherent text

Read the authentic text

Before reading the article printed below, see if you can work out the order in which these events occurred:
- El yate salió el jueves.
- Hubo un fallo del compás.
- El yate volvió el lunes.
- Iban a hacer unas compras.
- El jueves por la noche iniciaron el regreso.
- Salió para Fuerteventura.
- Las autoridades de Marina iniciaron las operaciones de búsqueda.
- Debía volver el viernes.
- Salió desde Las Palmas.

Write out the sentences in the correct order. You will find that you have a story that needs to be tidied up. Try to do this by cutting out any unnecessary repetition and adding any necessary connectors. Now read the text printed below and compare the story it tells with your own story.

Las Palmas de Gran Canaria
Regresó a puerto un yate tras haber sido dado por desaparecido
Un yate, que salió el jueves desde Las Palmas para el sur de Fuerteventura, a donde tenía que haber llegado el viernes, y que fue dado por desaparecido anteayer, regresó ayer a Gran Canaria.

Según declaró a la agencia Efe su propietario y patrón, Miguel Angel Ramos Mendoza, «todo se debió» a un fallo del compás que les daba un «rumbo falso» y que los acercó, «casi, a la costa africana».

Se trata del yate «Dachkaesfchawdag», de 9 metros de eslora, adquirido en Fuerteventura, concretamente en Morro Jable, por Ramos Mendoza a un alemán y que lo dedica a su uso particular.

El miércoles día 8, Ramos Mendoza, su compañera y sus dos pequeños hijos, decidieron venir desde Fuerteventura a Las Palmas para hacer unas compras «porque aquí las cosas están más baratas».

El jueves por la noche iniciaron el regreso, llevando como «invitado» a un joven, pariente de un amigo de la pareja, que pretendía buscar trabajo en la zona turística de Fuerteventura.

En una travesía normal, la embarcación debía haber llegado en la mañana del viernes a Morro Jable, y no lo hizo.

No obstante, quienes esperaban al joven invitado en Fuerteventura empezaron a inquietarse hasta el punto de denunciar la «desaparición» del yate a las autoridades de Marina en la tarde del domingo.

Las autoridades de Marina de Gran Canaria y Fuerteventura iniciaron las operaciones de búsqueda del yate en las costas de estas islas, con resultado negativo.

Cuando en la mañana de ayer la Comandancia de Marina iba a solicitar los servicios de un avión del SAR se advirtió, en el muelle deportivo, la presencia del yate que, según el celador de la Junta del Puerto, entró de madrugada.

Ramos Mendoza explicó que «todo se debió» a un «rumbo falso» que le daba el compás del yate, que los alejó más de la cuenta del rumbo previsto para dirigirse al sur de Fuerteventura.

Discussion of Example 11

Example 11 is based on the belief that the process of ordering the nine sentences will activate the learner's world knowledge about the sea, boats and accidents, and that this will facilitate his comprehension of the authentic report of an accident at sea. When he reads the authentic text the learner cannot help but match it against the target-language scenario he has already constructed. What is more, this process should also facilitate learning, since new material is being presented within a fully elaborated context of meaning, thus making it easier for the learner to associate new knowledge with what is already known.

(ii) Organizing vocabulary

The processes involved in Example 11 may well lead to effective learning; but the learner still needs a fair degree of grammatical and (especially) lexical knowledge in order to attempt the exercise with anything approaching confidence. Of course, it is possible to overcome this difficulty by introducing the exercise with a brain-storming session on relevant vocabulary. Example 12 effectively does this, combining work on vocabulary with the creation of a scenario that will provide a framework within which to encounter and respond to the authentic text.

Coping with the problem of vocabulary the learners do not know

EXAMPLE 12

Preparatory task: make up a story from a jumble of phrases

Working in pairs or small groups, invent a story using as many as possible of the following phrases:

ambas de 25 años - tras tomar unas copas - dos mujeres que sirvieron de gancho - en la calle Valvrede de Madrid - le dejaron en libertad - la policía arrestó a las dos parejas - un cuarto de hora - según informa - robar dinero, ropa y un reloj - dos hombres - intimidaron al visitante - llevaron a cabo el asalto

Read the text

Now read the following article and compare it with your own story.

El País, 21.11.87

Dos mujeres llevaron a un hombre a su casa para robarle

El País, **Madrid**

Dos mujeres que sirvieron de *gancho,* y otros dos hombres que llevaron a cabo el asalto, fueron detenidos ayer acusados de robar dinero, ropa y un reloj a un hombre de 46 años, según informa la Jefatura Superior de Policía de Madrid.

María Nieves Cabrera y Dolores Monge Guillén,

ambas de 25 años, conocieron en la calle Valverde de Madrid a un hombre al que tras tomar unas copas con él, le llevaron a una casa de la barriada del Pozo del Huevo, en Entrevías. Cuando apenas llevaban un cuarto de hora en su interior, siempre de acuerdo con el relato policial, entraron en la casa Miguel Angel González Marcos, de 27, y Francisco Javier Melero Ballesteros, de 26, quienes intimidaron al visitante con un objeto contundente y al que robaron el reloj, una cazadora de cuero, un talonario de cheques y una tarjeta de crédito. Posteriormente le dejaron en libertad.

La policía, tras recibir la llamada del asaltado, hizo un rastreo por la zona y arrestó a las dos parejas, recuperando todo el botín.

(iii) Productive exercise chains

Examples 13 and 14 briefly compared with Examples 11 and 12

Examples 11 and 12 both involve the learner in predictive activity that is productive in a limited way. Examples 13 and 14 take this a stage further and place the authentic text at the end of a chain of activities involving the learner in more fully elaborated productive activities.

EXAMPLE 13

Preparatory tasks: sort jumbled nouns and verbs into categories according to meaning; create a story from the combinations of nouns and verbs; re-order jumbled sentences

(a) Here is a jumble of VERBS and NOUNS:

Polizei - Taucher - liegen - finden - Diebstahl - Menge - Hotel - stehlen - hinunterhoppeln - Touristen - Auto - Grund des Rheins - prüfen - anziehen - Parkplatz - kommen - versinken - anrufen - Versicherung - zurückdrängen - Treppe - Kranwagen - Auto - Rheinufer - Zeuge - denken - hieven - Feuerwehr - Wagen - melden - Handbremse

Which verbs and nouns can be linked together?

(b) Try to create a story from your combinations of nouns and verbs. You will need to include information about WER?, WO?, WANN? and WAS?

(c) Re-order the following thirteen sentences to make an accident report:
- Der Wagen versank allmählich.
- Die Polizei und die Feuerwehr kamen zum Rheinufer.

49

- Zwei Taucher fanden das Auto.
- Das Paar sagte, sie hätten die Handbremse angezogen.
- Sie wollten den Diebstahl einem Polizisten melden.
- Der Polizist sagte, das Auto lag auf dem Grund des Rheins.
- Die Versicherung wird die Sache prüfen.
- Mit dem Kranwagen hievten sie das Auto aus dem Wasser.
- Sie drängten die Menge zurück.
- Der Zeuge lief zum Hotel, um die Polizei anzurufen.
- Sie dachten, es sei gestohlen.
- Ein Zeuge erzählte, dass das Auto die Treppe zum Rhein hinuntergehoppelt sei.
- Zwei Touristen kamen zum Parkplatz am Rheinufer zurück und fanden ihr Auto nicht mehr.

edit story created from nouns and verbs;

(d) Go back to your own story and edit it, paying particular attention to verb forms, agreement of nouns and adjectives, and word order.

read text

(e) Now read the following newspaper report:

Allgemeine Zeitung, 21.9.87

Die Suche nach dem versunkenen Auto auf dem Rheingrund

Als das Paar aus Ahrweiler zum Parkplatz am Rheinufer zurückkehrte, war sein Auto verschwunden. Gestohlen sei es, dachten sie. Im selben Moment nahmen sie den Menschenauflauf an der Theodor-Heuss-Brücke wahr. Sprang dort ein Mensch in die Fluten, um sich das Leben zu nehmen? Die Wahrheit erfuhren die beiden Touristen wenige Minuten später von einem Polizisten, dem sie den Diebstahl melden wollten: das Auto aus Ahrweiler lag auf dem Grund des Rheins. Was war geschehen? Ein Augenzeuge berichtete, er habe auf der Treppe am Ufer gelesen, als es plötzlich neben ihm schepperte. Im nächsten Augenblick hoppelte ein nagelneuer Citroën dem Rhein entgegen, Stufe für Stufe, mit viel Schwung. Niemand hätte ihn halten können.

Der Wagen tauchte zuerst mit dem Heck ins Wasser, trieb dann ab, schwamm eine Weile und versank allmählich. Gerade noch konnte der erschrockene Leser erkennen, dass niemand in dem Auto sass. Auch die Kennzeichen konnte er sich merken. Dann sprintete er in ein nahegelegenes Hotel, um die Polizei zu verständigen, ein Portier telefonierte für ihn, trotz anfänglicher Zweifel.

Am Ufer sammelte sich schnell eine Menge Schaulustiger, ebenso auf der Theodor-Heuss-Brücke. Polizei und Feuerwehr drängten die Leute am Ufer zur Seite, die Wasserschutzpolizei sperrte eine Spur des Fahrwassers. Zwei Segler zeigten die Stelle, an der sie den Citroën zuletzt sahen. Die beiden Taucher, Norbert Fuchs und Hans Keiner, stiegen über den Leiterwagen hinab in die Fluten. Binnen zwanzig Minuten, die wie eine Ewigkeit wirkten, orteten sie das Auto und banden es fest. "Es lag 15 Meter entfernt aus vom Ufer in 3,50 m Tiefe", berichtete Norbert Fuchs später. Das Wasser war zu dem Zeitpunkt 22 Grad warm, die Strömung aber gewaltig wie stets. Mit Stahlseil und Seilwinde hievte die Feuerwehr den Wagen an die Oberfläche. Ölblasen quollen auf und zerplatzten zu kleinen, schillernden Teppichen. Der Kranwagen nahte, die Taucher banden zwei Schlaufen um das Auto. Kranfahrer Wilfried Jahres hob es behutsam an, Sturzbäche strömten aus dem Inneren des Citroëns. Doch halt! Der Wagen drohte aus den Laschen zu kippen. Kommando zurück, die gleiche Arbeit nochmals. Diesmal gelang es; die beiden Pechvögel aus Ahrweiler hatten ihr Auto wieder, durchnässt und verbeult. Sie trugen's mit Fassung.

Sie sagten, sie seien sicher, die Handbremse angezogen zu haben. Die Versicherung wird den Badeausflug des Autos prüfen, das abgeschleppt wurde. Ein Fremder fragte die beiden freundlich: "Kann ich Sie irgendwohin fahren?" Doch höflich lehnte das Paar ab.

EXAMPLE 14

Preparatory tasks: sort a jumble of nouns into categories; make simple sentences using the above nouns and these verbs

(a) Ci-dessous une série de substantifs en vrac. Mettez-vous à trois ou quatre et arrangez les substantifs en plusieurs catégories.

le moteur - la mer - le corps - le hors-bord - le voilier - les copains - le mât - le port - les blessés - le propriétaire - un passager - l'hélice - le pilote - le pont

(b) Faites des phrases simples à l'aide des substantifs ci-dessus et des verbes suivants:

avoir - fracasser - foncer - entendre - déchiqueter - voir - s'effondrer - masser - passer par-dessus bord

write a simple
story outline;

use the
authentic text
to correct or
improve the
story outline

Le Parisien,
21.8.87

(c) Vous avez le titre: "Le hors-bord fracasse le voilier".
Maintenant essayez de fabriquer une version simple du
scénario de l'histoire.

(d) Lisez maintenant l'article suivant et corrigez ou
améliorez votre scénario selon le cas.

Chauffards de la mer, encore un drame
Le hors-bord fracasse le voilier: 2 morts, 4 blessés
*Les six copains auraient décidé une sortie nocturne, et
ils ont vu l'étrave sauvage leur foncer dessus.*
NICE: Catherine COUSIN
Quand ils ont vu foncer droit sur eux le hors-bord fou, juste
à sortie du port de Beaulieu, Véronique, Bernard, Thierry
et trois copains, massés sur le pont de leur petit voilier, ont
hurlé: «Mais arrêtez! Arrêtez!» Avec le grondement du
moteur de 200 ch. le pilote du «Star-Galaxy» n'a ni entendu
ni vu les signes de détresse. Le choc a littéralement
fracassé le «Barbajacou» et projeté à la mer Pascal
Manini, vingt-quatre ans, déchiqueté par l'hélice du bateau harponneur. Brisé net, le mât du voilier - un six mètres
- s'est effondré sur un autre passager, Alex Vorelly, vingt-
quatre ans, actuellement dans un état très critique. Dans
le choc d'une violence inouïe, un jeune marin suédois du
«Galaxy» est passé par-dessus bord. Son corps n'a été
retrouvé qu'hier matin, par 16 mètres de fond.

«Il était 22 h 30. On venait de dîner sur le bateau, au
port, et quelqu'un a eu l'idée d'une petite balade en mer, à
la fraîche», raconte Bernard Sidler, l'un des rescapés
miraculeusement indemne.

- On n'a pas vraiment eu le temps de se rendre compte»,
précise son copain Thierry Delettre, un jeune Parisien en
vacances. «C'était à un mille à peine au large. On avait
pourtant nos feux de position.» Excès de vitesse incontest-
able, grave faute d'inattention et manque de maîtrise de
cette vedette rapide, annexe d'un yacht ancré à Saint-
Jean-Cap-Ferrat, le «Galaxy». C'est son propriétaire,
René Herzog, homme d'affaires suisse mais dont la
société est à Londres, qui avait pris les commandes. A ses
côtés, deux marins, un jeune Anglais, Nicholas Cuttelle,
qui s'en tire sans une égratignure, et Robert Kirid, le
Suédois.

Prévenus du drame par le sémaphore de Beaulieu, les
secours s'organisaient très vite, mais il est trop tard pour
Pascal Manini, employé de banque à Villefranche.
Véronique Bolinowski, vingt et un ans, la seule fille du

groupe, souffrant d'un hématome à la tête, et Pascal Pan-izzi, légèrement blessé à une main, n'étaient, eux, hospitalisés que quelques heures.

Discussion of Examples 13 and 14

The technique of having learners approach an authentic text via the creation of a text of their own perhaps takes the deliberate activation of existing knowledge as far as it is useful to go. It is important to emphasize that this technique was devised to facilitate the twin processes of comprehension and learning and not as a new way of getting learners to write essays in the target language. In the first instance the texts that they produce must be judged for their usefulness as comprehension aids and not condemned as hopelessly deficient attempts at pastiche (this is not to say, of course, that a particularly promising scenario should not be further edited into a well-finished text in its own right). In Chapter 1 we quoted two examples of texts produced by learners still in the early stages of coming to grips with French; and we saw how, for all their morpho-syntactic fragmentariness, those texts revealed a relatively sophisticated approach to the subject matter in question. It seems to us likely that the technique illustrated in examples 13 and 14 can greatly speed up the growth of the learner's interlanguage; and it is of course on a broadly based interlanguage that the development of more refined linguistic skills depends.

3.4 Productive activities

Avoid a rigid division of language skills according to exercise type

Although we have so far been concerned with exercises designed to promote learning through the comprehension of authentic texts, most of the examples we have given involve the learner in some kind of productive activity, especially if the target language is predominantly the language of classroom management and instruction. This should warn us against assuming too rigid a division of the language skills according to exercise type. At the same time, the communicative competence that we want our learners to develop in

53

interaction with authentic texts should include the capacity to go beyond reception to production, to give linguistic expression to their response to the authentic text. Thus it is entirely appropriate that we should want some of our learners' work with authentic texts to have oral or written production of the target language as its explicit goal.

Authenticity and productive activities

In keeping with the general principles of our approach, outlined in Chapter 2, we shall want our learners' productive activities to be authentic - concerned with the purposeful communication of meaning. Authenticity in this dimension is a particularly slippery concept. In order to do justice to the social reality of the target language on the one hand and our classroom on the other we should perhaps recognize

Two orders of authenticity

two basic orders of authenticity. The first order has to do with the classroom as a place where learning takes place within a unique structure of social relationships; whereas the second order has to do with the target language community and the contexts in which our learners may use the target language when they are not in the classroom. Clearly, there are points at which the two orders of authenticity overlap - for example, in a well-realized role play based on spoken or written production. But there are also points at which learners may be involved in activities which are entirely authentic in terms of the first order but largely inauthentic in terms of the second - for example, when they write an essay in the target language; the point being that writing essays is an activity largely limited to classrooms and a very small class of journalists and profes-

Keeping the two orders of authenticity in balance

sional writers. As far as the development of the learners' communicative competence is concerned, the two orders of authenticity must be held in careful balance. Learners need to learn how to behave in the target language community by practising some of the roles they are likely to be called on to play; at the same time the classroom can offer a whole range of activities that have no equivalent in the world outside but will help them to consolidate what they learn by other means.

The ability to speak and (more especially) write fluently in a foreign language is a very substantial achievement, and it is unlikely that learners will develop productive skills rapidly or easily. Perhaps the biggest single fault to be found with traditional approaches to the teaching of productive skills is that they provide learners with far too little assistance. The classic instance of this is the homework essay: in many instances the title is the only help that learners get, so that they are all too likely to construct what they want to say in English and then try to translate it into the target language - with predictable results. The great virtue of using authentic texts as the basis of productive exercises is that they provide learners with thematic, discourse, grammatical and lexical frameworks within which to work.

Traditional approaches to teaching productive skills give learners inadequate support

(i) Rewriting texts

Examples 15 and 16, both originally the culmination of exercise chains similar to those in Examples 13 and 14, require the learner to rewrite an authentic text. It is for the learner to determine how far he will attempt to depart from the structures of the original. Since a large part of the justification for basing productive activities on authentic texts lies in the help such texts provide, it is sensible to encourage learners to remain as far as possible within the limits of what they are confident they can get right. In terms of both learning value and motivation, it is good for learners sometimes to attempt something simple in the knowledge that they will get it right.

Encouraging learners to stay within the limits of their competence

EXAMPLE 15

Le Parisien,
16-17.1.88

FELIX LA CHATTE GLOBE-TROTTER

En vingt-neuf jours, une chatte a parcouru plus de 280 000 km! Elle a traversé trois continents. Pas à pattes, bien sûr, mais dans la soute d'un avion de la Panam, où elle se trouvait incognito.

A l'origine, la chatte, qui se nomme Félix, devait arriver le

3 décembre à l'aéroport de Los Angeles (Etats-Unis), après avoir fait le voyage avec sa maîtresse, Janice Kubecki, depuis Francfort. Mais sa cage avait été retrouvée vide. Finalement, Félix a été capturée dans le compartiment à bagages après plusieurs trajets. «Nous ne savons pas ce qu'elle a mangé», a déclaré un porte-parole de la compagnie, qui a écarté d'office la présence de souris clandestines dans l'avion.

Félix est maintenant en quarantaine à Londres, et attend que sa maîtresse revienne la chercher. En plus du voyage, elle devra rembourser les frais de procédure, qui se montent à 7 500 F.

Rewrite the authentic text, changing some of its central features

After a chain of activities similar to those in examples 13 and 14, comes the following:

Après avoir lu le texte, rédigez un article intitulé "Le chien qui a parcouru l'Irlande".

EXAMPLE 16

Le Matin,
5.10.87

Trempolino remporte l'Arc de Triomphe devant les anglais

Les bookmakers anglais n'ont vraiment pas de chance. Ils n'avaient que deux solutions perdantes dans l'Arc de Triomphe: ou le succès de REFERENCE POINT, grand favori de la course, sur lequel s'étaient abattues des pluies de livres sterling ces derniers jours, ou celui du français TREMPOLINO, monté par l'idole des petits turfistes britanniques, Pat Eddery, offert à 14/1. Débarrassés de bonne heure de REFERENCE POINT, ils devaient jubiler, mais leur joie a été de courte durée. Surgissant comme un diable de sa boite, leur bête noire TREMPOLINO s'envolait vers un succès évident ...

REFERENCE POINT, fidèle à son habitude, avait pris le train à son compte dès le départ, talonné par SHARANIYA qui avait manifestement pour mission de le faire sortir de ses gonds. NATROUN suivait tout près, suivi par ORBAN, TRIPTYCH, TABAYAAN, tandis que GROOM DANCER, TREMPOLINO et l'italien TONY BIN se désintéressaient le plus possible de la course. Avec où sans SHARANIYA, REFERENCE POINT se fût sans doute rendu de toute manière. Il l'a fait très tôt, peu après l'entrée de la ligne droite, et tous ceux qui l'avaient accompangé cédaient. TRIPTYCH elle même, la courageuse, la dure à cuire, demandait de l'oxygène.

A trois cent cinquante mètres du but, très intelligemment monté par Dominique Boeuf, GROOM DANCER tentait sa chance au meilleur endroit de la piste, le long du rail. Feu de paille. On sait maintenant qu'il ne tient pas, même par bon terrain. Simultanément, en pleine piste, TREMPOLINO trouvait facilement le passage, et accélérait en toute quiétude, vainement poursuivi par l'italien TONY BIN. Les attentistes avaient eu largement raison des plus impétueux. Il en va souvent ainsi à Longchamp dans les courses qui «roulent», comme disent les turfistes.

Pat Eddery remportait en l'occasion son quatrième Arc, égalant le record codétenu par Freddy Head, Yves Saint-Martin et Jacques Doyasbère. Mieux encore, il est le seul jockey à avoir remporté trois Arcs consécutifs (l'an passé DANCING BRAVE, il y a deux ans RAINBOW QUEST).

TREMPOLINO était le seul concurrent appartenant à un propriétaire français, ce qui n'a pu que réjouir le président de la République, venu hier aux courses pour la première fois de son septennat. François Mitterand a eu la chance de découvrir Longchamp par une belle journée d'automne, ce qui n'avait pas toujours été le cas pour ses prédécesseurs.

DANIEL LAHALLE

Rewrite the authentic text so that the race follows a different pattern from the one reported

Parcourez le texte et notez la manière dont la participation de chaque cheval est décrite. Ensuite, lisez le text. Trempolino a gagné. Mais, imaginez que Reference Point ait gagné la course! A l'aide des phrases que vous avez déjà repérées dans le texte, décrivez cette course imaginaire. Essayez autant que possible de changer le rôle de la plupart des concurrents.

Editing target language texts as a language learning technique

If undertaken with an appropriate degree of preparation, the act of editing or transposing an authentic text will involve the learner in much analysis of the grammar of the original as well as its thematic and lexical content. In view of the importance that teachers and examiners traditionally attach to grammatical and orthographical accuracy, it is rather odd that editing text has not been more widely recommended as a language learning technique. After all, it involves developing and practising precisely those skills on which accuracy of written production depends. The same skills are deployed in the correction of written work: the essential difference between learners on the one hand and teachers and examiners on the other is not that the latter have necessarily superior powers of invention, but that they have much more highly developed editing skills. This provokes the thought that just as learners may profit more from devising than from answering traditional comprehension questions, so they may learn more from correcting one another's work than from looking through their own work after it has been corrected by the teacher.

(ii) Authentic texts and formal letters

Letter-writing and the second order of authenticity

Rewriting or transposing authentic texts is an activity that belongs firmly in the classroom, and thus to our first order of authenticity. Writing letters, on the other hand, is something that learners will need to do if they aspire to contact with their target language community; letter-writing thus belongs to our second order of authenticity.

Letter-writing conventions

Each language has its own conventions for the lay-out of letters, which can be particularly important in more formal communication. Learners need as part of their communicative survival kit a basic model of the formal letter that they can adapt to a variety of purposes. Example 17 provides such a model in German, the purpose of the authentic text - in this case a series of advertisements for summer courses - being to provide the learner with the pretext for writing the letter. The substance of the authentic text is included in the instructions given to the learner.

EXAMPLE 17

Material on holiday courses: a letter-writing task

Schreibe einen Brief an die Kurverwaltung, 2242 Büsum. Bitte um Informationen zu dem Web- und Spinnkurs: Kosten, Daten, Übernachtung/Frühstück, Unterkunft, Anzahl der Stunden; bitte um eine Broschüre.

An die   .....
Kurverwaltung   .....
...   .
          den .....

Sehr geehrte/r ...,

Ich interessiere mich für ...
Könnten Sie mir bitte ...
Ich bedanke mich im Voraus für Ihre Mühe.

Mit freundlichen Grüssen

...

(iii) Authentic texts and personal letters

The difference between personal and formal letters

Personal letters differ from more formal correspondence in much the same way as casual, free-wheeling conversation differs from (say) a business meeting: to a considerable degree rhetorical structure is a matter of personal preference and tends to be much less important than content. Accordingly, once learners are in command of the basic conventions of letter-writing in their target language (lay-out, how to begin and end), they need help chiefly with content. Thus Example 18 is another exercise in text editing and transposition disguised as a letter-writing exercise; however, unlike Examples 15 and 16, the target text belongs to our second order of authenticity - it is a role play.

EXAMPLE 18

A letter-writing task

You are spending a week in the youth hostel in Wangerooge. Write a letter to your exchange partner in Hamburg describing Wangerooge, its youth hostel, and the things you do each day. Make as much use as you can of the material contained in the texts printed below.

Material from tourist brochures

WANGEROOGE
am Eingang zum Jadebusen ist die östlichste der Ostfriesischen Inseln. Ihre Geschichte ist sehr wechselvoll. Nachdem Wangerooge bereits 1327 Stadtrechte erhielt, lebten seine Bewohner bis zum Jahre 1818 mal unter russischer, niederländischer und französischer Herrschaft. Knapp 2000 Einwohner leben hier. Zu den Sehenswürdigkeiten der Insel gehört ein Naturschutzgebiet. Für den guten Rundblick bieten sich der Westturm und der Leuchtturm im Nordwesten der Insel an.
Bahnreise bis Sande, von dort mit dem Bus bis Harle zum Übergang aufs Schiff. Von Wangerooge Westanleger zum Ort fahren Sie mit der Inselbahn.
Deutsche Bundesbahn, Schiffsdienst und Inselbahn Wangerooge, 2944 Wittmund 2, Telefon: (0 44 69) 2 17.

Jugendherberge Wangerooge "Westturm"

Lage des Hauses: Der Turm - das Wahrzeichen Wangerooges - liegt am Westende der Insel und ist zu Fuss vom Anleger am Strand entlang in 20 Minuten zu erreichen. Bahnhof ist 45 Minuten entfernt.

Geeignet für: Einzelgäste, Ferienfreizeiten, Schulklassen, Schullandheimaufenthalte und Sportgruppen.

Freizeitangebote: Kirchen, Leuchtturm, Reitstall, Fahrradverleih und kulturelle Veranstaltungen. Um den Gästen reine Luft und Ruhe zu bieten, sind benzinbetriebene Fahrzeuge (mit Ausnahme von Krankenwagen und Feuerwehr) auf der Insel nicht gestattet. Möglichkeiten der Freizeitgestaltung: Führung ins Watt oder Vogelschutzgebiet, Krabbenkutterfahrt zu den Seehundsbänken, Nachbarinseln, evtl. Festland- sowie Helgolandfahrten, Fernsehen. Grillplatz am Haus. Ein bewachter Badestrand ist 200 m von der Jugendherberge entfernt.

Bankverbindung: Landeszentralbank Oldenburg, Zweigstelle Wangerooge Nr. 053-403 101, BLZ 280 501 00.

Nächste Jugendherbergen: Carolinensiel, Jever, Schillighörn.

Bitte beachten: Die Jugendherberge ist von Mai bis September geöffnet. Genauen Anfangs- und Schlusstermin bitte erfragen. Anreise nur nach Voranmeldung möglich. Der Aufenthalt ist kurtaxpflichtig und nur in Verbindung mit Vollverpflegung möglich. Träger Landesverband.

Different forms of *curriculum vitae*

(iv) Curricula vitae

Letters apart, a *curriculum vitae* is perhaps the text type that it is most useful for language learners to be able to produce. In all European cultures the *curriculum vitae* can take a number of forms, depending on the purpose it is intended to serve; these range from the extremely skeletal and schematic at one extreme to the discursive potted autobiography at the other. If they are provided with an appropriate model even learners in the earliest stages should be able to compile a *curriculum vitae* of the former kind - as instanced already in Example 9. Example 19 provides a further illustration.

EXAMPLE 19

Quick, 53/87

Zwei Leben - ein Schicksal
44 Jahre wussten die Zwillinge Gerda Roleff und Erika Wagner gegenseitig nichts von ihrer Existenz. Jetzt trafen sie sich durch Zufall wieder. Und stellten trotz der langen Trennung verblüffende Gemeinsamkeiten fest. Bis hin zu ihren Kindern und Krankheiten.

Heute lachen sie über diese "dumme Sache". Und sehen sich mitten im Lächeln ernst an. Und sie sagen gleichzeitig und mit demselben Tonfall, jede das Echo der anderen: "Ein bisschen unheimlich ist das Ganze schon."

Die "dumme Sache" stiess den beiden Frauen zur gleichen Zeit zu: eine Blinddarmoperation.

Beide wussten damals nichts von der Existenz der anderen: Die eine lag in Berlin in der Klinik, die andere in Leipzig. Aber beide ärgerten sich: "Warum muss das ausgerechnet im Sommer passieren, wo alle Welt zum Baden geht?"

Zufall, dachte sich Erika Roleff in Berlin. Und in Leipzig tröstete sich Gerda Wagner: "Das ist eben Zufall ..."

Es war kein Zufall, sondern unbeeinflussbare Bestimmung. Eine Bestimmung, die beiden Frauen schon zum Zeitpunkt der Zeugung in jeder Körperzelle mitgegeben worden war. Erika Roleff und Gerda Wagner sind eineiige Zwillinge.

Aber das haben sie erst jetzt erfahren, nach 44 Jahren, als sie sich in Augsburg wiedertrafen. Aber diesmal wirklich durch einen Zufall ...

Die beiden wurden am 7. Juli 1939 als Gerda und Erika Wegener in Berlin-Karlshorst (heute DDR-Gebiet) geboren. Während der Bombennächte 1943 kam Gerda - damals vier Jahre alt - mit Lungenentzündung ins Krankenhaus. Wegen der Luftangriffe wurde sie eines Nachts Hals über Kopf mit allen anderen Patienten nach Leipzig evakuiert.

Beim Transport ging das Namenbändchen an ihrem Handgelenk verloren.

Aus dem Krankenhaus kam die kleine Gerda in ein Leipziger Waisenhaus, später zu einer Pflegefamilie. 1978 zog sie nach Augsburg.

Ihre Zwillingsschwester Erika war mit den Eltern in Berlin geblieben. Verzweifelt suchten die Eltern jahrelang mit Hilfe des Roten Kreuzes, den Aufenthaltsort ihrer verschollenen Tochter Gerda zu finden. Ergebnislos.

Verständlich, dass sich Gerda bis zu dem zufälligen Treffen in Augsburg für eine Waise hielt. Denn erst jetzt, nach 44 Jahren, trat Zwillingsschwester Erika wieder in ihr Leben, als Gerda ein Pfund Kaffee kaufen wollte und in ein Geschäft in der Augsburger Innenstadt trat.

Die Kaffeeverkäuferin sprach sie sichtlich erfreut an: "Hallo, Tante Erika, wie geht's?" Gerda Wagner antwortete überrascht: "Was soll das? Ich kenne Sie nicht, ich bin nicht Ihre Tante."

Jetzt war die Verkäuferin, Lilo Wegener, 32, bestürzt. Wenn diese Frau, die genauso aussah und sprach wie ihre Tante Erika Roleff in Berlin, die sogar die gleiche Brille trug wie sie, nicht ihre Tante war - wer war sie dann? War diese Frau vielleicht die verschollene Zwillingsschwester?

So war es, so kam es zum Wiedersehen. Und dann feierten die Zwillinge. Mit einer Flasche Krimsekt. Und erzählten einander die Stationen ihrer getrennten Vergangenheit - zwei Schicksale mit erstaunlichen Übereinstimmungen.

Zuerst die Blinddarmoperation. Beide wie aus einem Mund: "Das war im Sommer 1962."

Erika: "1969 musste ich wieder ins Krankenhaus. Eine Operation an der rechten Brust ..."

Gerda zuckte zusammen: "Bei mir war 1969 das gleiche. Alles ging gut - aber jetzt plagen mich seit Jahren Migränenanfälle."

Erika: "So ein Zufall - mir geht's genauso."

Gerda brachte sieben Kinder zur Welt, auch Erika war siebenmal schawanger. Und noch mehr Gemeinsamkeiten. Beide tragen seit vielen Jahren die gleiche Kurzhaarfrisur, beide haben die gleichen Sehschwächen, beide tragen am liebsten Hosen und Pullis, beide lieben Operettenmusik.

Da sprach keine mehr von Zufall.

Complete this curriculum vitae:

Name:	Erika Wegener
Geboren:	7. Juli ...
Geburtsort:	
Aufgewachsen in:	
Krankheiten:	
im Alter von:	... Jahren
Kinder:	

Now write a curriculum vitae for (a) Gerda and (b) yourself.

(v) Speaking activities

Like the writing activities we have considered, speaking activities based on authentic texts can be

Speaking activities and the two orders of authenticity

categorized according to our two orders of authenticity. On the one hand there are activities that belong to the world of the classroom and form a continuum with the use of the target language as medium of classroom management and instruction; the learners' elicitiation of one another's views, discussions, and debates fall into this category. On the other hand there are simulations that are focussed on one or another aspect of the target language culture - learners may, for example, act out roles suggested by the authentic text. It is fundamental to the whole argument of this book that learners will get more out of authentic texts the more thoroughly they are encouraged to interact with them. Speaking activities based on authentic texts should be treated in the same way, which means that a discussion or role play is likely to succeed in proportion as it is thoroughly prepared - involving the learners in various kinds of lexical, grammatical, discourse and thematic analysis. Example 20 shows how an authentic text can be used to rehearse a conditional structure that is specially relevant to discussion of the theme "free time"; this is done not for its own sake, however, but as preparation for a class survey and discussion.

The importance of appropriate preparation

EXAMPLE 20

Bunte, **10.9.87**

FREIZEIT

Alexandra ist in der Oper, Anja hat Probe, Dagmar gibt Turnunterricht und Manfred ist - wenn überhaupt - zwischen elf und zwölf zu erreichen. Nachts. Eines verbindet diese Teenager zwischen 15 und 19: Sie haben Terminkalender wie Top-Manager.

So wie Dagmar Neusser aus Düsseldorf. "Freitag ist der schlimmste Tag", sagt Dagmar und strahlt dabei. Denn "schlimm" heisst lediglich ausgefüllt. Wenn freitags die Schule um halb zwei aus ist - und für Millionen von Arbeitnehmern das lange Wochenende beginnt -, geht's für Dagmar erst richtig los. Von der Schule hetzt sie zu ihrem Job als Turntrainerin, danach hat sie Italienischkurs, und dann geht's noch zur Jazztanzgruppe. Nach gut zwölf Stunden Hektik kommt sie um neun nach Hause. Dort warten noch einmal zwei Stunden Hausaufgaben auf sie.

Die Psychologin Dr. Katharina Holzheuer vom Evangelischen Beratungszentrum in München kennt solche

Stundenpläne aus ihrer Praxis. "Neben der Schule existieren eine Menge Aktivitäten, die sehr häufig leistungsorientiert absolviert werden." Nach ihrer Erfahrung wird Rumhängen als Belastung erlebt. Action ist angesagt, und dafür werden auch Unannehmnlichkeiten in Kauf genommen.

Anja Beckert aus Saarbrücken ist erst fünfzehn, doch ein Ziel hat sie schon ganz fest im Visier. "Ich will Opernsängerin werden. Es sei denn", schränkt sie ein, "meine Stimme trägt nicht." Seit die Gymnasiastin als Chorsängerin in Humperdincks "Hänsel und Gretel" auf der Bühne stand, liebt sie das Theater im allgemeinen und die Oper im besonderen.

Als Statistin am Saarländischen Staatstheater muss sie Disziplin und Pünktlichkeit beweisen. Nachmittags hat sie Probe für eine Neuinszenierung, am Abend Vorstellung. Sie hat bei rund hundert Aufführungen mitgewirkt, Proben nicht mitgerechnet.

Fühlt sie sich nicht manchmal gestresst? Sie schaut mich nach dieser Frage an, als wolle ich sie beleidigen. Stress, was ist das? Schliesslich bleibt ihr ja immer noch genügend Zeit, ihren Brieffreunden in Kanada, Schweden, Spanien, Kenia, Peru, Frankreich und der DDR (uff!) zu schreiben, Klavierstunden zu nehmen und zum Jazztanz zu gehen. Ach ja, und in einer Jury, die Stücke für ein Schülertheater-Festival aussucht, sitzt das zarte Kind auch noch.

Das einzige, was ihr in letzter Zeit auf den Magen geschlagen sei, "ist die Sache mit der Schülerzeitung an meinem Gymnasium". Weil es mit der Teamarbeit im Redaktionskollektiv nicht mehr klappte, hob Anja mit sieben Gehilfinnen eine Konkurrenzzeitung aus der Taufe. Und ganz nebenbei gehört sie auch noch zu den Besten ihrer Klasse.

Alexandra von Prittwitz, Dekorateurlehrling in München, hatte mit Schule nie viel am Hut. Doch an ehrgeizigen Plänen mangelt es auch ihr nicht. Ihr Ziel: einmal als Möbeldesignerin in New York zu leben. Sie ist selbstbewusst und optimistisch.

Nix "No future", obwohl sie wie ein Punker aussieht: Die Haare lila, grün und rosa gescheckt, Jackett und Hose sehen aus, als stammten sie aus einer DRK-Kleidersammlung. Nur ihre Manieren sind äusserst gepflegt. "Ich stehe in der U-Bahn auf und biete einer alten Dame meinen Platz an. Und ich mag es, wenn mir jemand die Tür aufhält, mir in den Mantel hilft."

Alexandra raucht nicht, trinkt am liebsten Kakao und

hört mit Leidenschaft Beethoven. Nach ihrem Acht-Stunden-Tag im Kaufhaus geht sie in die Oper oder zu Vernissagen.

Ihr Motto: Man muss nicht alles studiert haben, aber man muss viel ausprobieren, mitmachen, um zu wissen, wo die eigenen Stärken liegen. So ging sie gegen ein geringes Entgelt als Au-pair-Mädchen nach England, öffnete Austern bei einem Münchner Feinkosthändler und half bei Partys, durstigen Gästen die Gläser zu füllen. "Alles, was ich mache, bringt mich meinem Ziel ein Stückchen näher", so ihre Überzeugung, "und mein Ziel bin ich selbst."

Preparation for discussion: practising conditional constructions

Diskutieren Sie, ob Sie auch so viele Freizeitbeschäftigungen haben möchten.

BEISPIEL: Wenn Sie Zeit hätten, würden Sie auch in die Oper gehen?

Bilden Sie weitere Fragen nach diesem Muster:
1. eine gute Stimme haben - Opernsängerin werden
2. nur vormittags Schule haben - nachmittags Italienischkurs machen
3. kein Geld haben - durstigen Gästen Gläser füllen
4. Platz in der U-Bahn - älterer Dame anbieten
5. Zeit haben - Beethoven hören

A classroom survey

Umfrage in der Klasse: Was machst du in der Freizeit?

Examples 21 and 22 introduced

Example 21 has as its culminating activity a simulated interview with Ivan Beshoff, last survivor of the Potemkin mutiny. As with the various writing activities described above, so here the authentic text is thoroughly processed before the role play is attempted. The fact that the first three activities could equally well be used to prepare for a written task should again warn us against assuming that most learning activities are tied to one particular language skill. Our last illustration in this section, Example 22, underlines this point: the brief authentic text provides the stimulus and content for a survey of how learners spend their free time; the survey is conducted orally in Spanish; and the results of the survey are then used to rewrite the Spanish text. In this instance the blending of language skills is accompanied by a merging of the two orders of authenticity to give what is potentially a deeply satisfying chain of activities.

EXAMPLE 21

Le Monde,
29.10.87

Le dernier survivant du cuirassé «Potemkine» est mort en Irlande

Le dernier survivant connu de la mutinerie du cuirassé *Potemkine*, M. Ivan Beshoff, est décédé dimanche 25 octobre, à son domicile de Dublin.

M. Beshoff était ingénieur-mécanicien à bord du *Potemkine*, cuirassé de la flotte impériale russe de la mer Noire, lorsque l'équipage se révolta, le 14 juin 1905, après l'exécution d'un matelot par un officier.

L'armada russe avait alors reçu l'ordre d'attaquer le *Potemkine* et de mater la rébellion, mais les équipages des autres bateaux avaient refusé de tirer sur leurs camarades.

Dans un entretien récent, Ivan Beshoff, membre à l'époque du Parti social-démocrate russe, expliquait qu'il s'était alors enfui clandestinement en Angleterre, où il avait rencontré Lénine. Puis, avec d'autres mutins, il avait gagné l'Amérique du Sud avant de s'établir définitivement en 1913 en Irlande, où il a d'abord travaillé pour une société pétrolière soviétique. Il y a été arrêté deux fois, accusé d'espionnage au profit de l'Union soviétique. Après la seconde guerre mondiale, il avait ouvert un florissant restaurant de «*fish and chips*» (poissons et frites) à Dublin.

Explain selected words contained in the authentic text; read the text and replace the words with your definitions; consider how the sense of the text has been changed; work out an interview based on the authentic text

1. Expliquez les mots suivants avant de lire l'article: Potemkine; Lénine; mer Noire; flotte impériale; mutinerie; cuirassée; matelot; armada. Vous pouvez, si nécessaire, utiliser un dictionnaire.

2. Lisez l'article. Maintenant remplacez dans l'article (oralement ou par écrit) les mots de la liste précédente par les définitions que vous avez trouvées.

3. Le sens du texte est-il le même? Si ce n'est pas le cas, demandez au prof. de vous aider à trouver des définitions plus précises.

4. Divisez la classe en groupes de deux. A l'aide du plan ci-dessous, imaginez un interview de M. Ivan Beshoff.
   (a) Journaliste: demande à M. Beshoff de se présenter (âge, origine, etc. ...)
   (b) M. Beshoff: réponse
   (c) Journaliste: demande à M. Beshoff où il se trouvait en 1905 et ce qu'il faisait
   (d) M. Beshoff: réponse

EXAMPLE 22

em, 11/87

¿Y tú qué haces?

Según las últimas encuestas, los jóvenes de los Pirineos hacia abajo escogen para su tiempo libre estas alternativas: salir con los amigos (calle, bares ...), 79%; ver TV o video, 63%; escuchar música, 60%; salir de copas, 53%; lectura, 42%; cine, 34%; radio, 30%; deporte, 28%; excursiones camprestres, 22%; espectáculos deportivos, 20%; salir con el novio/a, 19%; tocar un instrumento musical, 12%; actividades políticas, 9%; asociaciones recreativas, 7%; teatro, 7%; otras, 5%. «Dime qué haces cuando no haces nada y te diré quién eres».

Conduct a classroom survey in Spanish and use the results to rewrite the authentic text

Conduct a survey in Spanish among your classmates to see how they spend their leisure time. Ask questions like:

¿Cuántas veces por semana sales con tus amigos?

¿Practicas algún deporte?

¿Vas muy a menudo al cine?

When you have finished, rewrite the Spanish article, replacing the results of the original survey with your own results.

3.5 Learning vocabulary and grammar from authentic texts

Meaning and form interdependent

In Chapter 2 we argued that because in any language meaning and form are inseparable, a central part of our purpose should be to discover means of enabling learners to understand more acutely how the forms of their target language are organized in the creation of meaning.

Vocabulary and grammar central concerns in many of the above examples

Vocabulary and grammar are central concerns of many of the activities illustrated in sections 3.3 and 3.4. For example, the more elaborate exercise chains begin with a preparatory activity that focuses on the analytical organization of vocabulary; while activities that require learners to edit or rewrite text inevitably bring grammar into the foreground. It is important to note that the presence of the authentic text guarantees that work on grammar and vocabulary is always contextualized: morphosyntactic forms and word meanings are always treated in relation to larger units of communication.

Authentic texts provide a context of meaning for work on vocabulary and grammar

Whereas texts are included in most traditional foreign language courses because they introduce a particular area of vocabulary and/or illustrate a particular grammatical point, in an approach based on authentic texts grammar and vocabulary are analysed because they are relevant to an understanding of the text in question.

However, we do not wish to give the impression that there is nothing more to successful language learning than working through exercises of the kind illustrated in this chapter, based on a more or less random selection of authentic texts. The demands and constraints that a formal educational context imposes will always make it necessary to underpin unconscious processes of acquisition with a deliberate effort of conscious and analytical learning. Among other things this means that all learners need to keep track of target-language vocabulary and grammar in carefully organized notebooks.

The need to underpin unconscious processes of acquisition with a deliberate effort to learn; hence the need for carefully organized notebooks

One of the most important claims implied in this chapter is that learners can be helped to understand an authentic text by first working on a jumble of words taken from the text in question. Organizing vocabulary into an outline story or description should also make it easier to remember: research into how memory works suggests that we find it easier to remember something if we encounter it as part of a larger unit of meaning rather than as an isolated item; while research into language processing has shown that we do not store words in memory randomly but in association with other words.

Organizing vocabulary makes it easier to learn

Learners' notebooks should include the fruits of all the word-categorization exercises that they perform in their work on authentic texts, together with vocabulary-building exercises of a related but independent type: networks of word-roses constructed around basic themes like "school", "house and home", "hobbies", that draw on the resources of authentic texts as they become available. It is vitally important that vocabulary should be recorded in an organized way, and no less important that the learners themselves should do the organizing since this is an essential part of the

Organizing vocabulary notebooks

Using authentic texts to build vocabulary

Using authentic texts to come to terms with similarities between L1 and L2

Getting learners to devise and correct exercises for one another

Learning grammar by manipulating authentic texts

learning process.

Authentic texts can also be used as the basis for more random vocabulary-building activities. For example, learners can be required to scan all the headlines in a newspaper, or perhaps a whole page of text, in order to find particular words - equivalents of English words or synonyms for target-language words. This can be done against a time limit so as to encourage learners to develop scanning skills. In Chapter 1 we discussed some of the advantages and disadvantages that arise for language learners from similarities between their own and the target language. Learners can be encouraged to come to terms with the problems that such similarities pose by having them work through an authentic text finding as many words as possible that look like English words and then working out which are close cognates and which are not. But however random the means by which new vocabulary is discovered, it should always find its place in the overall organization of the learner's vocabulary notebook.

At various points in this chapter we have suggested that learners may usefully devise and correct exercises for one another. This is especially the case with exercises that are focussed on vocabulary and grammar. An authentic text can rapidly be turned into various kinds of cloze exercise. For example, whole words can be deleted in order to raise issues of synonymy, antonymy and collocation; alternatively, the inflexional system can be brought into focus by deleting only inflexional endings. Learners can also set one another exercises that involve the rewriting of authentic texts: a third-person text can be transposed into the first person and vice versa; or a text written in the past can be transposed to the present. Finally, learners can discover much about the syntax of their target language by reducing compound sentences to their component propositions and by combining simple declarative propositions into compound sentences. We return to some of these issues in the next chapter.

3.6 Conclusion: getting it all together

Putting authentic texts at the centre of language learning

At present most teachers use authentic materials to supplement a language course book. However, the arguments that we elaborated in Chapters 1 and 2 carry the implication that authentic texts should be the centre around which all other language learning materials are organized. Authentik has plans to develop various kinds of support material for both teacher and learner that should make this easier to achieve; but in the meantime teachers who want to construct their course on authentic texts must assume a considerable burden of organization.

Any attempt to implement the pedagogical techniques that we have presented in this chapter must take account of the practical constraints that impose themselves on every course of language teaching. To begin with there are the constraints that arise from the

Constraints imposed by the educational system

educational system. First language acquisition is a highly intensive process that engages the child for a large proportion of its waking hours; and the difference between first and "naturalistic" second language acquisition lies less in the intensity of the process than in the fact that the second language learner may be able to withdraw between times to a first language environment, for example by returning to his family at

The problem of insufficient intensiveness

the end of the working day. By contrast, foreign language teaching in formal educational environments is traditionally a matter of very small doses administered over a relatively long period. This must create difficulties for the activation of natural acquisition processes, and it challenges teachers to use all their ingenuity to keep the learners' attention focussed on the target language. No doubt the question of a more intensive approach to language teaching should be at the centre of any thoroughgoing overhaul of the post-primary curriculum; but in the meantime teach-

The limitations imposed by the length of lessons

ers have to find ways of coping with the situation as it is. Many of the activities we have been concerned with in this chapter not only require time in their own right

70

but also lead naturally into further activities, and it is difficult to maintain momentum if every lesson comes to an end after forty minutes. Some teachers may be able to counteract this to the extent of arranging for each of their classes to have at least one double period each week. The choice of homework activities is also crucial in maintaining continuity.

**Homework
and continuity**

The learners themselves are a second source of constraints. Even supposing that our classes are composed of learners with a higher than average level of interest who present no discipline problems, we still face the fact that the attention span of even the most committed learners is limited: there is always the risk that boredom will set in before they get to the end of a particular activity. It is specially important to bear this in mind when learners are being led through a chain of activities based on a single authentic text. The people who devised the chain were no doubt sustained by the challenge that this process made to their ingenuity, and it probably never occurred to them that learners could become bored long before reaching the end of the chain. In general learners are more likely to succeed if they have a clear sense of purpose which enables them to organize their thoughts and learning activities efficiently. This is another reason why they should be encouraged to become as autonomous as the systems permits; and once again homework has a crucial role to play.

**Constraints
that arise from
the learners**

**Limitations of
attention span**

**The need
for a sense
of purpose**

Further constraints arise from the teacher's limited preparation time. It is one thing to understand the principles on which an exercise is based, but quite another to find the time to devise quantities of exercises sufficient to keep a class of thirty learners occupied for four lessons a week throughout the school year. No doubt this is why most teachers use ready-made exercises. However, one of the central convictions of this chapter is that the most effective language learning may be based not on exercises that take hours to devise and minutes to do, but rather on activities that take very little

**Constraints
arising from
the teacher's
limited
preparation
time
One solution:
get learners to
devise and
correct
exercises**

time at all to prepare but quite a long time to perform. At various stages in this chapter we have suggested that learners themselves might learn as much from devising exercises as from doing them; obviously this technique can be deployed to relieve some of the pressure on the teacher.

The biggest constraint of all: public examinations

But perhaps the biggest constraint of all is the one imposed by the public examinations. Objections to pedagogical innovation frequently take the form: "That's all well and good in theory, but it's nothing like the exam my learners have to pass." We attach such importance to this issue that we have given it a chapter of its own.

Suggestions for further reading

Two books by H. G. Widdowson contain a wealth of ideas that can be applied to authentic texts: *Teaching Language as Communication* (already mentioned at the end of Chapter 2) and *Stylistics and the Teaching of Literature* (London: Longman; 1975). The communicative exercise typology developed by German applied linguists and language teachers at the end of the 1970s likewise contains many ideas that can readily be adapted to authentic texts. It has been published in several forms, including *Übungstypologie zum kommunikativen Deutschunterricht*, by G. Neuner, M. Krüger and U. Grewer (Langenscheidt: Munich; 1981) and *The Communicative Teaching of English*, edited by C. N. Candlin (London: Longman; 1981). Another rich source of material on classroom activities relevant to work with authentic texts is *Communication in the Modern Languages Classroom*, by J. Sheils (Strasbourg: Council of Europe; 1988).

Readers interested in finding out more about recent work on vocabulary should consult *Vocabulary: Applied Linguistic Perspectives*, by R. Carter (London: Allen & Unwin; 1987) or *Vocabulary and Language Teaching*, edited by R. Carter and M. McCarthy (London: Longman; 1988).

W. Rutherford and M. Sharwood Smith have edited a useful collection of readings on different aspects of grammar in language teaching: *Grammar and Second Language Teaching* (Rowley, Mass.: Newbury House; 1987). *Grammar in Action*, by C. Frank and M. Rinvolucri (London: Prentice Hall International; 1987) and *Teaching Grammar*, by S. McKay (London: Prentice Hall International; 1987) are a useful source of practical suggestions for contextualized grammar work.

Three CLCS Occasional Papers (published by the Centre for Language and Communication Studies, Trinity College, Dublin) discuss issues closely related to the central concerns of this chapter: No.18 - *Learning a foreign language through the media*, by S. Devitt; No.20 - *Authentic materials and the role of fixed support in language teaching: towards a manual for language learners*, by D. Little and D. Singleton; and No.21 - *Classroom discourse: its nature and its potential for language learning*, by S. Devitt.

Chapter 4

Authentic texts, exercise types and public examinations in Ireland

Purpose of this chapter: preparing learners for exams

However it is achieved, successful language learning is the best preparation for language examinations; and sustained work on authentic texts is as likely as any other approach to give learners the level of formal accuracy that examiners demand. After all, for learners in the classroom authentic texts can fulfil the same kind of function as the community of native speakers fulfils for the person learning a foreign language "naturalistically"; and language acquisition research has found that the grammar of a language is acquired as a result of sustained interaction in and with the language in question. It nevertheless seems to us useful to make more explicit the relationship between authentic texts and language learning exercises of the kind presented in Chapter 3 and the tasks that are set in the Leaving Certificate exams in French, German and Spanish.

Structure and content of this chapter

The chapter begins by charting the tasks to be performed at both Higher and Ordinary levels for each language, and goes on to analyse the different components of the processes of reading and writing. These different components are then linked explicity to each examination task, thus yielding a clear idea of what components require special attention for each task. After a brief discussion of cloze tests, the remainder of the chapter illustrates practical techniques for developing each separate component. Three texts, one each for French, German and Spanish, serve as the basis for the exercises proposed at each stage. The French and German texts are taken from past issues of *Authentik*, the Spanish text from the 1987 Leaving Certificate Higher Level paper, where it was given for translation into English. We have done this in order to show that the principles we are concerned to elaborate are applicable to texts that actually appear in examinations and to the tasks associated with them.

Same pedagogical approach in this chapter as in the rest of the book

We should perhaps emphasize that the same pedagogical approach underlies this chapter as the rest of the book. The exercise types that we suggest are often similar, sometimes identical, to those illustrated in Chapter 3, but they are dealt with from the point of view of examinations. Furthermore, while the actual tasks to be performed vary from one language examination to another, the skills required for these various tasks do not differ greatly. Thus most of our proposals are applicable to more than one type of task.

4.1 Analysis of examination tasks

An analysis of the tasks set in the 1987 Leaving Certificate examination papers yields Tables 1 and 2 (the letter/number combinations given in square brackets at the top of each entry indicate the section and question numbers on the relevant examination paper).

Differences between tasks set in different language exams

The differences between the tasks being set in each language are immediately obvious. For example, only the Spanish papers have translation and only the Spanish Higher Level paper has prescribed literary texts, though these are optional; Spanish does not have the cloze tests found in French and German at both levels; and German is unique in having the "compositional exercise". Other differences are: the language used for questions in comprehension tests; the type of question (multiple choice or open); the nature of the questions (whether they are precise, relating to specific points in the text, or more general). Similarly the amount of information candidates are given about the content and the format to be observed in written tasks varies considerably from one paper to another.

One interesting difference between French and German which Tables 1 and 2 do not highlight is the treatment of cloze tests. On the German papers these

TABLE I

LEAVING CERTIFICATE EXAMINATIONS 1987

**QUESTIONS RELATED TO READING COMPREHENSION
IN FRENCH (FR), GERMAN (GE) AND SPANISH (SP)**

H = Higher Level; O = Ordinary Level

Tasks

CL1	Cloze test;
CL2	"Cloze" test focused solely on grammar.
Com1	Comprehension/appreciation of literary text.
Com2	Comprehension of general texts.
Com3	Appreciation of prescribed literature.
T1	Translation from target language to English.

Exams and levels

Tasks	FR/H	FR/O	GE/H	GE/O	SP/H	SP/O
CL1	[I,Q.1] Instructions in French	[I,Q.1]	[1 c] Instructions in English	[1 c]		
CL2			[4 b] Coherent text; words (verbs) given			[D i] Single sentences; multiple choice
Com1	[II, Q3] Qs.in French; multiple choice		[I a] Qs.in English; precise		[B 4] Qs.in English; general	
Com2	[II Q.2] Qs. in French; multiple choice	[II a,b] Qs. in (a) Fr, multiple choice; (b) Eng precise	[I b] Qs. in English, precise	[I a,b] Qs. in English, precise	[B. 5] Qs.. in English, general	[B i,ii] Qs. in (i) Eng, precise; (ii) Sp, multiple choice
Com3					[B 1-3] (Optional)	
T1					[D]	[D ii]

TABLE 2						
LEAVING CERTIFICATE EXAMINATIONS 1987						
QUESTIONS RELATED TO WRITTEN PRODUCTION IN FRENCH (FR), GERMAN (GE) AND SPANISH (SP)						

Tasks

C.ex Compositional exercise (composing longer units from simple sentences)

L Letter writing

R Report or message writing, based on notes

O Expressing opinions, with or without guidelines

N Narrative

T2 Translation from English to target language

	Exams and levels					
Tasks	**FR/H**	**FR/O**	**GE/H**	**GE/O**	**SP/H**	**SP/O**
C.ex			[4] Format: parag. of four complex sents. from 12 sents.	[4 a] Format: sentences - five complex sents. from 5 pairs.		
L	[III Q4,5] Formal & informal; format: n.given; content: given in Fr & Eng	[III] Formal & informal; format: n.given; content: given in Fr & Eng	[2] Informal; format: given; content: given in German mainly	[2] Informal; format: given; content: given in German mainly		[C i] Informal; format: given; content: given in Spanish
R	[III Q.6] Content: notes in French			[3] Content: notes in English		
O	[III Q7] Format: article/ letter/ diary; content: given in Fr (topic)		[3] Format: article; content: given in Ge (notes)		[C i] Format: letter/ conver- sation; content: given in Sp (text) & English	[C ii] (Optional) Format: conver- sation; content: given in Sp (topic)
N					[C ii]	[C iii] (Optional)
T2					[A]	[A]

French and German exams treat cloze tests differently

constitute the final question in the section dealing with reading comprehension; they are clearly considered to be testing the candidate's understanding of the text. On the French papers, on the other hand, cloze is given a section of its own. This would seem to indicate a certain lack of decision about what exactly is being tested - reading comprehension or written production. In fact, as we shall see below, both are being tested.

German exam: "elaboration of notes" as expression of opinion

Finally, teachers of German may be surprised to find that we have included the section on the Higher Paper entitled "Elaboration of Notes" in our category "Expressing opinion". It is obviously the examiners' intention that candidates should write a text that closely follows the guidelines given for format and content. Yet there is more freedom here for personal expression than in other sections; indeed, candidates are explicitly instructed to give personal opinions. It seemed appropriate, therefore, to group this task with the French and Spanish questions which seek candidates' opinions. The effect on the task of giving strict guidelines will be examined below.

Exam papers fall into two broad divisions: reading and writing

At this stage it should be clear that the examination papers fall into two broad divisions, tests of reading comprehension and tests of written production. It is to a consideration of what these two skills entail that we now turn.

4.2 Model of reading and writing

It is not possible here to discuss theories of reading or writing in any detail. Instead, we shall present a model of these processes, taking into account the various components of relevant theories. The model is presented schematically in Table 3.

Model related to principles outlined in Chapters 1 and 2

Our model is closely related to the principles outlined in Chapters 1 and 2, especially the principle that all language learning takes place within a framework of knowledge of the world and knowledge of discourse types. In our model these two frameworks

Result	Linguistic knowledge	Other knowledge
TABLE 3 **COMPONENTS OF READING AND WRITING PROCESSES**		
Writing Production of a grammaticalized text		
	2b Syntax beyond the sentence (e.g. discourse markers, use of pro-forms, etc.)	
	2a Morpho-syntax of basic sentence (e.g. word order, morphology etc.)	
Reading Finding the message of a text		
Writing Transmitting a message through a text in telegraphic form but with correct discourse structure		**0b** Knowledge of discourse
	1 Vocabulary stores (including information about words, their networks) [Linguistic data bases]	**0a** General knowledge frameworks (world knowledge, knowledge of the topic)

are given on the right hand side and are numbered 0a and 0b respectively. They are what the learner (even the child learning its first language) brings to the task.

However, in order to communicate we need various levels of linguistic knowledge. We take the basic level (1) to be the vocabulary store. As we noted in 2.3 and 3.5, much of our world knowledge is recalled and referred to in words. An important part of the child's development in its first language is the building up of a vocabulary store, and the same is obviously true of a second language. This component consists of words stored in various ways - primarily, perhaps, according to semantic fields or meaning-relatedness. Gradually the vocabulary store comes to include a mass of information about words - their probability of occurrence, the other words they most frequently associate with, the networks of relationships between them, as well as more and more information about their semantic value.

Vocabulary store as basic level of linguistic knowledge

Primitive discourse created from vocabulary store

With this basic level of linguistic knowledge we can create discourse. We illustrated this in Chapter 1 with two texts produced by learners of French (see p.8 above). In each case the learners either possessed already or created from their world knowledge the components of what happened (0a); they then matched the vocabulary they had been given or already possessed (1) to the components of the event; and they used their knowledge of discourse structure (0b) to create their own texts, to transmit a message.

Basic level of linguistic knowledge, schemata, and the comprehension of texts in an unfamiliar language

Several of the exercises included in Chapter 3 show how this basic level of linguistic knowledge allows us to comprehend texts in an unfamiliar language. Our starting point may be familiar words, words already stored in our memory; alternatively it may be some non-linguistic element like a photograph or a map. From either starting point we can evoke a certain schema of knowledge, and there will be movement backwards and forwards between the words on the page and the schema, each adding to and refining the other. The less familiar we are with the language the more intensive will be this movement between words and schema as we try to match them and go on to discover the discourse structure which gives the message of the text. As we grow in linguistic knowledge this process is speeded up; we have more information in our vocabulary stores to draw on, but the basic components remain the same, as does our basic purpose: the discovery of the message.

Morpho-syntactic knowledge at sentence level and above

Moving upwards in the model we come to the final components, which consist of morpho-syntactic knowledge both at sentence level (2a) and beyond (2b). We stressed in Chapters 1 and 2 that this stage is reached only gradually, that much of the process of language learning consists precisely of the grammaticalization of basic discourse, that is, the marking of the various elements of discourse according to the grammatical conventions of the language in question. This process of grammaticalization is again evident in the two French texts cited in Chapter 1: the boy did not have the linguistic ability to go beyond the level of basic discourse, whereas the four girls showed some progress in the development of their morpho-syntactic knowledge. Developing the skills required for written production requires detailed knowledge of this type. In comprehension this extra level of knowledge may be less important, providing us with further information to help us find the message of the text, but mainly in the form of checks. But both production and comprehension involve the same components and move in the same direction.

What is needed to develop each component of the reading/ writing model

We can now list what needs to be done to develop each component of the reading/writing model (numbers are those given to the different components in Table 3):

Comprehension

0a Develop the skill of using world knowledge.
Add relevant cultural knowledge for the target language to existing world knowledge.

0b   Develop the skill of using knowledge of discourse structure.
Add relevant information about specific target
language discourse structures.

1   Build up vocabulary store, especially in ranges
specified by the syllabus.
Build up information about the networks of associations between words and about what words combine with one another.

0a and 1   Develop the skill of relating vocabulary to world knowledge to create meaningful clusters.
Develop the skill of organizing the elements of these clusters to get to the message of the text.

2a and 2b   Develop the skill of using morpho-syntax and discourse markers to check the message.

Production

0a   Develop world knowledge in relevant domains.

0b   Develop the knowledge of target language discourse structures where relevant, e.g., for letters, both formal and informal, for reports, descriptions, narrative, etc.

1   Build up vocabulary store, especially in ranges specified by the syllabus. Build up information about the networks of associations between words and about what words combine with one another.

0a and 1   Develop the skill of relating vocabulary to world knowledge to create meaningful clusters.

0a, 0b and 1 Develop the skill of organizing the elements of these clusters to create meaningful text.

TABLE 4

COMPONENTS OF READING AND WRITING PROCESSES RELATED TO EXAMINATION TASKS

CL1	Cloze test
CL2	"Cloze" test focused solely on grammar
Com1	Comprehension/appreciation of literary text
Com2	Comprehension of general texts
Com3	Appreciation of prescribed literature
C ex:	Compositional exercise (composing longer units fromsimple sentences)
L	Letter writing
R	Report or message writing, based on notes
O	Expressing opinions, with or without guidelines
N	Narrative
T1	Translation from English to target language
T2	Translation from target language to English

Exam tasks

Components	CL1-2	Com1-3	T2	L	R,O,N,	T1	C ex
2b Syntax beyond the sentence	Develop for CL1	Use as check	Use as check	Develop	Develop	Develop	Develop
2a Syntax of simple sentence	Develop esp. for Fr/H	Use as check	Use as check	Develop	Develop	Develop	Given
1 Vocab. stores	Develop	Develop	Develop	Develop	Develop	Develop	Given
0b Knowledge of discourse structures	Use	Use	Use	Given in Ger. Develop in Fr/Sp	Given in Ger. Develop in Fr/Sp	Given	Given
0a Knowledge of world, topic	Use	Use	Use. in Fr/Sp	Given in Fr/Sp (Use in Ger)	Given (Use in Ger)	Given	Given
Skill of linking 0a and 1	Develop	Develop	Develop				

2a Develop morpho-syntacic knowledge at simple sentence level in order to edit texts.

2b Develop knowledge of syntax beyond the simple sentence and of the relevant discourse conventions and markers.

4.3 Model of reading/writing linked to examination tasks

An analysis of exam tasks in terms of the reading/writing model

These recommendations are embodied in Table 4, which brings together the information in Tables 1-3. In a number of the examination tasks certain of the components of our model are given, sometimes in detail. Thus we saw in Table 1, for example, that in the letter writing exercises the content was given at least partly in English on the French and Spanish papers; the German paper, on the other hand, required candidates first to decipher a text in German before writing; they would, therefore, have had to use the component of world knowledge for this task.

4.4 Some reflections on cloze tests

Before going on to suggest ways of developing the different skills in relation to the examination tasks, it is necessary to clarify some points in relation to cloze tests. We have already mentioned the differences that exist between the conception of cloze tests in the French and German examinations. Different skills appear to be required in the two languages.

What are cloze tests?

Cloze tests are constructed by deleting elements from a text and requiring the learner to insert an appropriate word or expression in each gap. In our examination system, these deletions are not random or even quasi-random (for example, every 7th or 10th word) but are made in such a way as to include a set range of grammatical categories. Thus, for example, in the French Higher Level examinations in 1986 and 1987, the following categories were tested:

Cloze tests in French Higher Level exams analysed

	1986	1987
Nouns	3	1
Verbs	4	2
Determiners	4	4
Pronouns	1	-
Conjunctions		4
Prepositions	4	7
Neg.particles	1	1
Adverbs	3	1
Total	20	20

Cloze tests can require world and discourse knowledge as well as linguistic knowledge

In cloze tests world and discourse as well as linguistic knowledge can have a role to play: some gaps can be filled only if we have an idea of what the text is about. In the French tests cited above seven items in 1986 and four or five in 1987 required this type of knowledge; for example: "Il a bien fallu que quelqu'un *s'occupe* des vignes." Other gaps demand a knowledge of how the text is structured, requiring the learner to know how to use *bien que* or *mais*. However, in both examinations referred to the majority of items demand precise grammatical knowledge only; for example, that *supérieur* and *avoir recours* are followed by the preposition *à*, or that "on fait *du* sport". For these items (well over half the total) the context provides very little help in deciding what the relevant item is; so that this is really a grammar test in cloze format.

Cloze in the 1987 French Ordinary Level exam

By contrast, the 1987 French Ordinary Level examination had a much higher proportion of items which required world knowledge or an understanding of the topic; in other words, the context was important in deciding what was missing. Examples were: "*entend* les bruits" (verb and direct object closely linked semantically); "*fermer* la fenètre ... et le murmure cesse" (choice suggested by the meaning of the latter part of the sentence). The German examinations at both levels contained a high proportion of items which required an understanding of the context.

Cloze in German exams

Preparing learners to do cloze tests: an alternative to practice tests

Obviously, the approach to be taken in preparing learners for cloze tests will vary according to the type(s) of skills being tested. Rather than give learners series of cloze tests and ask them to get on with them, in the belief that practice is all that is required, it seems more reasonable to isolate the different skills required and to develop them gradually through different types of exercises.

Skills needed to do a cloze test

What are these skills? At single word level the learner needs vocabulary; this may be specifically related to the topic of the text - for example, *cinema, film, screen, box-office,* - or may be general. At sentence level he needs to know what changes to make to the basic word in order for it to be morphologically and syntactically acceptable in the position in which it occurs. This demands a knowledge both of the appropriate forms and of their corresponding uses. The learner also needs to know how the different parts of a text relate to one another. For example, some of the deleted words may be explicit discourse markers, like *however* and *therefore*; others, for example pronouns, may contribute to the cohesion of the text in less obvious ways. In any case, most missing elements contribute to the coherence of a text in important ways and will therefore have to relate meaningfully with other elements in the text.

An example should help to illustrate the different skills required. Let us take the well-known fable of Aesop that we used in Chapter 1, first of all in telegraphic form:

A sample cloze test: basic version

Crow find cheese.
Crow eat cheese.
Fox see crow.
Fox praise (1) _____ of crow.
Crow sing.
Crow (2) ____ cheese.
Fox pick up cheese.
Fox run away.

To do this cloze test the learner must understand the text, decide on the meaning and function of the missing words (1: noun, belonging to crow, related to *sing*, direct object of *praise*; 2: verb, let fall) and retrieve the appropriate words *voice* and *drop* from his active vocabulary. In terms of Table 3, the components required are 0a (world knowledge) and 1 (vocabulary) only.

In a more elaborated form of the text this knowledge will still be required; in addition, however, the learner will have to be able to select the appropriate form of the words chosen. Here is a cloze test based on one of a set of variations on the theme by James Thurber:

A sample cloze test: elaborated version

A fox, attracted by the scent of something, followed his nose to a tree in which (1) _____ a crow with a piece of cheese in his beak. "Oh, cheese," said the fox (2)_____. "That's for mice."

The crow removed the cheese with his talons and said, "You always hate the thing you cannot have, as, for instance, grapes."

"Grapes are for the birds," said the fox haughtily. "I am an epicure, a gourmet, and a gastronome."

The embarrassed crow, ashamed to be seen (3)_____ mouse food by a great specialist in the art of dining, hastily (4)_____ the cheese. The fox caught it deftly, swallowed it with relish, said "Merci," politely, and trotted away.

Different kinds of knowledge and different kinds of error

In the case of the missing verbs, the learner has not only to know the correct words, but also their tense and the form in which to express that tense. If he writes *sit* for (1) he shows he has the correct meaning; *sitted* would indicate knowledge of the correct tense; while *sat* would indicate knowledge of meaning, tense and form. Either of the two "wrong" options does, therefore, show a certain level of linguistic competence which should be recognized. What of the option *eat* for *eating* in (3), or *droped* instead of *dropped* in (4)? And what about other options for *scornfully* in (2)? Relating this to Table 3 above, we again require components 0a and 1, but also 2a (morpho-syntactic knowledge at sentence level) and at least some 2b (syntax beyond the sentence) since the choice of tense depends on other elements in the text.

Definite and indefinite articles focus on syntax above sentence level

If we used the Thurber text to create a cloze test in which we omitted *a* before the first mention of *crow* in the first paragraph, *the* before the second mention of *fox* in the same paragraph, and *an* before *epicure* in the third paragraph, leaving a space also before *grapes* in the same paragraph, we would be getting learners to focus on a small closed set of words, the choice of which is almost totally dependent on the position within the discourse of the noun in question. The knowledge required for this task would be mostly 2b (syntax beyond sentence level), with some knowledge of syntax at sentence level if there were a question of grammatical agreement of article and noun. On the other hand, if the words omitted were prepositions, for example, *by*, *to* or *in* in the first paragraph, very little apart from some minimal morpho-syntactic knowledge (2a) would be required. It is obvious, therefore, that one must look very carefully at the cloze test that is actually being proposed in order to decide which skills the learner needs.

Prepositions focus on morpho-syntax

4.5 Developing the different components and skills

(i) Three sample texts

As we explained at the beginning of this chapter, we have chosen one text for each language as the basis for illustrating the practical techniques we propose for developing the different skills required for examinations. The French extract is taken from an article entitled "Victime de son courage", which appeared in

Le Parisien of 5 October 1987 and was published in *Authentik en Français* of November 1987. It deals with a man who helped save 27 children from a fire in Besançon and as a result developed a respiratory condition which caused him to lose his job; he was then threatened with eviction:

Sample French text

VICTIME DE SON COURAGE

En avril 1985, alors qu'un incendie ravageait son immeuble, Camille Tournier avait arraché vingt-sept adolescents du brasier. Gravement intoxiqué par la fumée il avait perdu son emploi. Aujourd'hui, alors qu'il est privé de ressources, et dans l'attente d'une opération, le gérant de son immeuble veut le faire expulser. Mais les locataires, reconnaissants, prennent sa défense.

... Ce jour-là, Camille Tournier, quarante et un ans, se précipite dans les couloirs de son bâtiment ravagé par un incendie. L'épaisse fumée produite par la combustion des matières isolantes a envahi la cage d'escalier où jouent habituellement les gamins.

Avec deux autres habitants de l'immeuble, Camille leur fraie un passage vers une trappe de secours: elle est condamnée par une chaîne! Il ne se désespère pas et, suivi par la petite troupe, il réussit enfin à pénétrer dans ·un appartement d'où les pompiers, avec une grande échelle, évacueront les vingt-sept enfants.

Cet acte de bravoure, Camille va le payer cher. Gravement intoxiqué par la fumée, touché au poumon, le coeur faiblissant, il doit être hospitalisé dans un état désespéré. La maladie ne l'emportera pas mais Camille Tournier devra pourtant ensuite abandonner son travail de surveillant de magasin. Ses absences répétées, dues à des malaises, ont lassé son employeur. Et Camille, qui a un enfant à charge, s'est bien vite retrouvé sans ressources...

The German text is an extract from the article about twins, "Zwei Leben - ein Schicksal", originally published in *Quick* Nr. 53/87 and already reprinted in Chapter 3. The article appeared in the February 1988 edition of *Authentik auf Deutsch*:

Sample German text

... Die beiden wurden am 7. Juli 1939 als Gerda und Erika Wegener in Berlin-Karlshorst (heute DDR-Gebiet) geboren. Während der Bombennächte 1943 kam Gerda - damals vier

Jahre alt - mit Lungenentzündung ins Krankenhaus. Wegen der Luftangriffe wurde sie eines Nachts Hals über Kopf mit allen anderen Patienten nach Leipzig evakuiert.

Beim Transport ging das Namensbändchen an ihrem Handgelenk verloren.

Aus dem Krankenhaus kam die kleine Gerda in ein Leipziger Waisenhaus, später zu einer Pflegefamilie. 1978 zog sie nach Augsburg.

Ihre Zwillingsschwester Erika war mit den Eltern in Berlin geblieben. Verzweifelt suchten die Eltern jahrelang mit Hilfe des Roten Kreuzes, den Aufenthaltsort ihrer verschollenen Tochter Gerda zu finden. Ergebnislos.

The Spanish text was given as a translation test on the 1987 Spanish Higher Level paper. Its source is not known.

Sample Spanish text

El 7 de junio de 1926, un anciano despistado, modestamente vestido y sin documentación alguna, es atropellado por un tranvía junto a la Plaza de Cataluña en Barcelona. Se le conduce a un hospital, donde nadie le conoce, ni consiguen saber quién es. Dos días después, poco antes de morir, por fin logran identificarlo: es ni más ni menos que Antoni Gaudí, el original arquitecto que había revolucionado artísticamente a la sociedad catalana.

Es el último cuarto del siglo XIX, cuando el joven Gaudí, originario de Reus (Gerona), procedente de una familia humilde de caldereros y que había sacado notas bastante mediocres en su carrera de arquitectura, comienza a dar sorpresas a sus conciudadanos.

Son los años dorados. Barcelona en aquella época es el centro de todo: los artistas proliferan y encuentran en esta ciudad su caldo de cultivo. Cataluña se industrializa, las ideas liberales y burguesas están en todo su pensamiento; y en la búsqueda del resurgir de la cultura catalana, aparecen movimientos como Renaixença, en donde Gaudí ocupa un lugar destacado.

El específico estilo de Gaudí es prácticamente irrepetible. Él no conoció el Modernismo, el Expresionismo ni el Superrealismo, pero los miembros de estos movimientos bien que le debieron conocer a él, ya que en determinada medida fue un poco su precursor.

90

(ii) Developing the vocabulary component

A systematic approach to vocabulary building

It is obvious from Table 4 that vocabulary is the component that needs to be developed right across the board. How should learners go about doing this? In Chapter 3 we suggested that they should store vocabulary in semantic fields rather than in random lists because this corresponds more closely with the memory's natural storage mechanism. An A3 scrapbook or art-pad is eminently suitable for this purpose, especially when Post-its are used for each new item (Post-its are small adhesive labels that can be attached to and removed from any surface as often as one wishes; they are particularly valuable for language exercises which involve moving linguistic elements around.)

Interlinking semantic fields

In order to work with the vocabulary of a particular text like the Thurber example quoted above we need to connect a number of semantic fields. A useful basic structure is one which interlinks sets of words for the key areas PEOPLE, PLACE, TIME, EVENT. It is possible to start by presenting words in a jumble as in Figure 1. The words can then be organized in clusters as illustrated in Figure 2. Note that words belonging to more than one set or semantic field are clustered in the intersections; also that here and in all succeeding figures we have adopted the convention of giving nouns in lower case, verbs in capitals, and adjectives and adverbs in italics.

Developing learners' knowledge of semantic networks

In Chapter 3 and again in this chapter we have stressed the need to develop learners' knowledge of the semantic networks to which words belong and their sense of what words can combine with what other words. Tables 5 and 6 show how this might be done for the Thurber text.

Applying our techniques to the sample texts

Figures 3-7 and Tables 7-13 show the application of these techniques to our French, German and Spanish texts. We have by-passed the basic vocabulary store, since it would be too cumbersome here to attempt to cover all the relevant fields. But for each text we show the process of clustering the vocabulary into meaning-

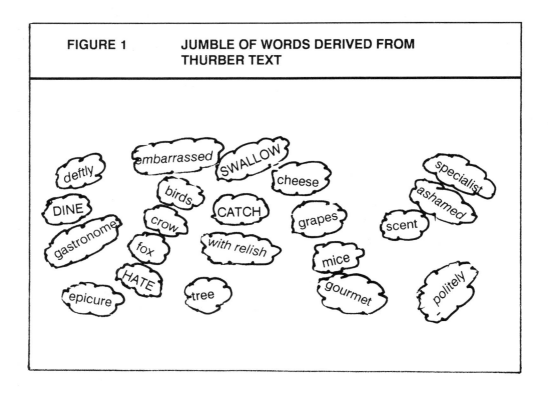

FIGURE 1   JUMBLE OF WORDS DERIVED FROM
            THURBER TEXT

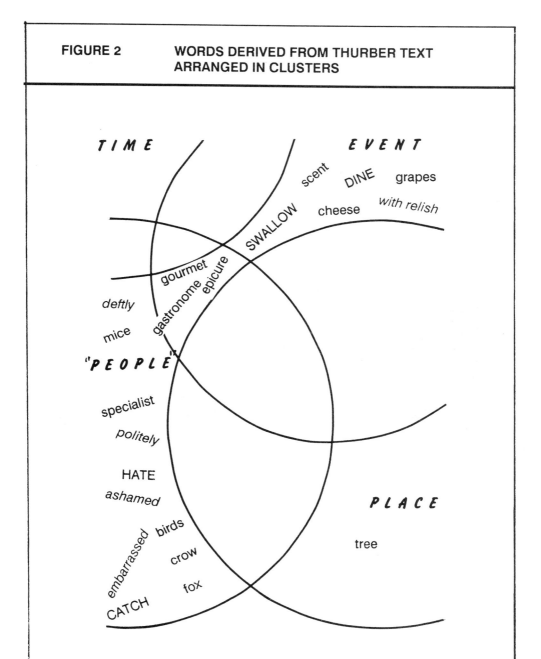

FIGURE 2   WORDS DERIVED FROM THURBER TEXT ARRANGED IN CLUSTERS

TABLE 5		THURBER TEXT: EXAMPLES OF SEMANTIC NETWORKS - NOUNS AND ADJECTIVES				
	clever	*embarr-assed*	*ashamed*	*deftly*	*politely*	*with relish*
fox	yes	yes	yes	yes	yes	yes
crow	yes	yes	yes	yes	yes	yes
birds	yes	yes	yes	yes	yes	yes
mice	yes	yes	yes	yes	yes	yes
tree						
cheese						yes
grapes						yes
talon						
beak						

TABLE 6		THURBER TEXT: EXAMPLES OF COLLOCATION POSSIBILITIES - NOUNS AND VERBS (X= subject, Y = object)				
	REMOVE	CATCH	HAVE	HATE	SAY	SWALLOW
fox	x	x/y	x	x/y	x	x
crow	x	x/y	x	x/y	x	x/y
birds	x	x/y	x/y	x/y	x	x/y
mice	x	x/y	x/y	x/y	x	x/y
cheese	y		y	y		y
grapes	y		y	y		y
talon	with	with	in			
beak	from	with	in			with

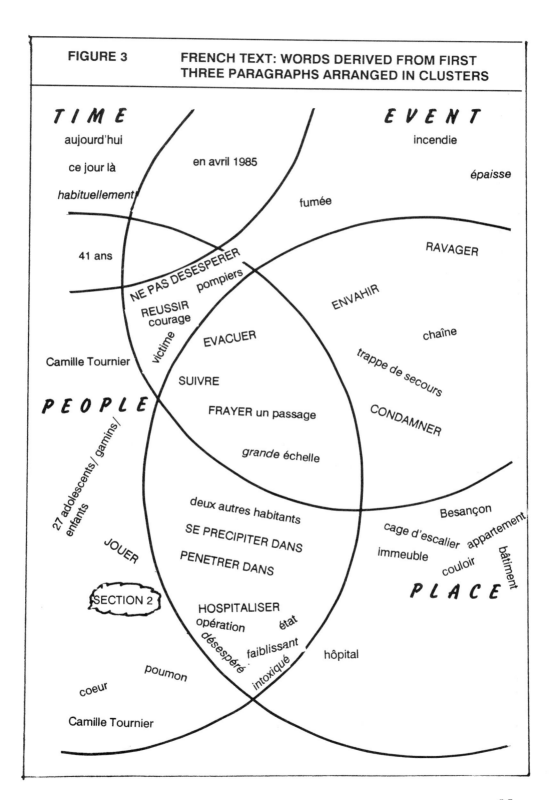

FIGURE 3 FRENCH TEXT: WORDS DERIVED FROM FIRST THREE PARAGRAPHS ARRANGED IN CLUSTERS

95

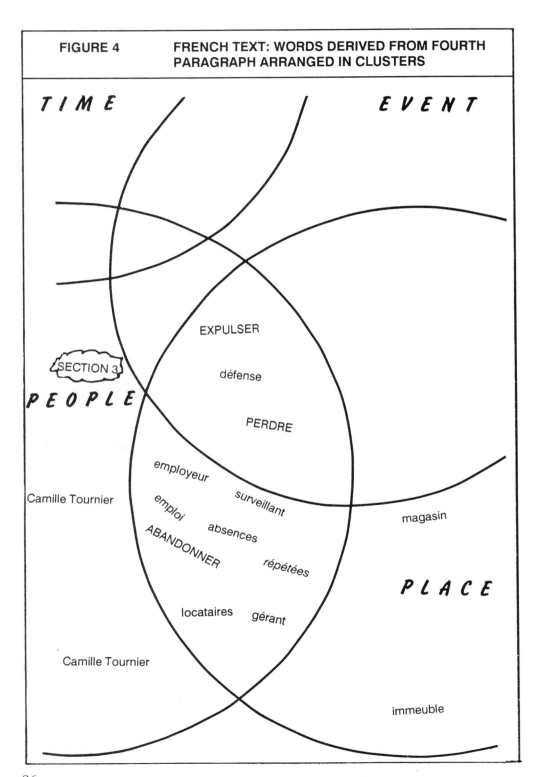

FIGURE 4   FRENCH TEXT: WORDS DERIVED FROM FOURTH
PARAGRAPH ARRANGED IN CLUSTERS

TIME

EVENT

EXPULSER

défense

SECTION 3

PEOPLE

PERDRE

employeur

surveillant

Camille Tournier

emploi   absences

ABANDONNER

répétées

magasin

PLACE

locataires   gérant

Camille Tournier

immeuble

TABLE 7	FRENCH TEXT: EXAMPLES OF SEMANTIC NETWORKS				
	mène une vie dangereuse	met sa vie en jeu	s'occupe de personnes	s'occupe d'affaires	s'occupe d'un immeuble
pompiers	oui	oui	oui		
gérant					oui
surveillant					oui
employeur				oui	
policier	oui		oui		
docteur			oui		
infirmière			oui		

TABLE 8	FRENCH TEXT: COLLOCATION POSSIBILITIES - NOUNS AND ADJECTIVES					
	grand	épais	intoxiqué	faiblissant	désespéré	répété
courage	oui					
fumée		oui				
incendie	oui					
échelle	oui					
appartement	oui					
couloir	oui					
immeuble	oui					
coeur				oui		
poumon			oui			
état					oui	
absence						oui

	payer un loyer	payer un salaire	louer un apparte-ment	évacuer	jouer
gamins					X
victime				Y	
pompiers		à Y		X	
locataires	X		X/à Y		
gérant	à Y		X		
adolescent					X
surveillant		à Y			
employeur		X			
policier		à Y		X	

TABLE 9
FRENCH TEXT:
EXAMPLES OF COLLOCATION POSSIBILITIES - VERBS & NOUNS
(X = subject, Y = object)

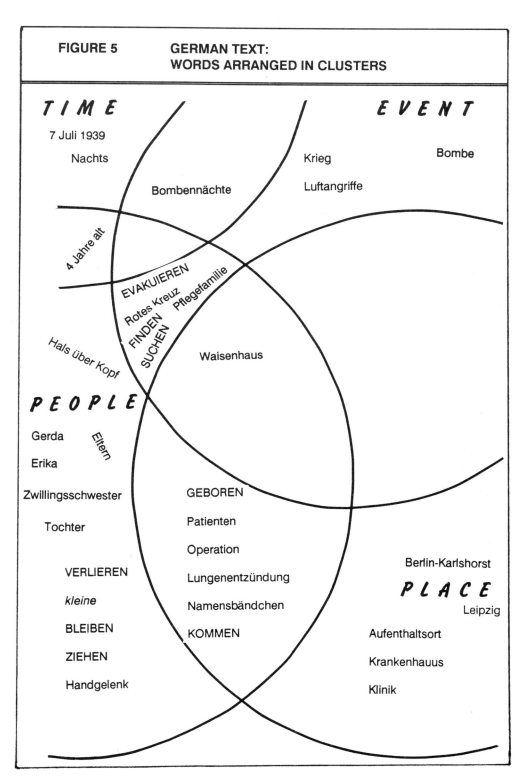

FIGURE 5   GERMAN TEXT: WORDS ARRANGED IN CLUSTERS

99

TABLE 10 **GERMAN TEXT: EXAMPLES OF SEMANTIC NETWORKS**

	jung	eineiig	ähnlich	mit dem Krieg assoziiert	mit dem Krankenhaus assoziiert
Eltern			ja		
Kinder	ja		ja		
Tochter	ja		ja		
Zwillinge	ja	ja	ja		
Pflege-familie				ja	
Patienten					ja
Rotes Kreuz				ja	ja

TABLE 11 **GERMAN TEXT: EXAMPLES OF COLLOCATION POSSIBILITIES - VERBS & NOUNS (X = subject, Y = object)**

	schwanger sein	zur Welt bringen	geboren werden	sorgen für	evakuieren
Eltern		X		X	
Frau	X	X		X	
Kinder		Y	X	Y	Y
Zwillinge		Y	X	Y	
Patienten				Y	Y
Pflegefamilie				X	
Rotes Kreuz				X	X

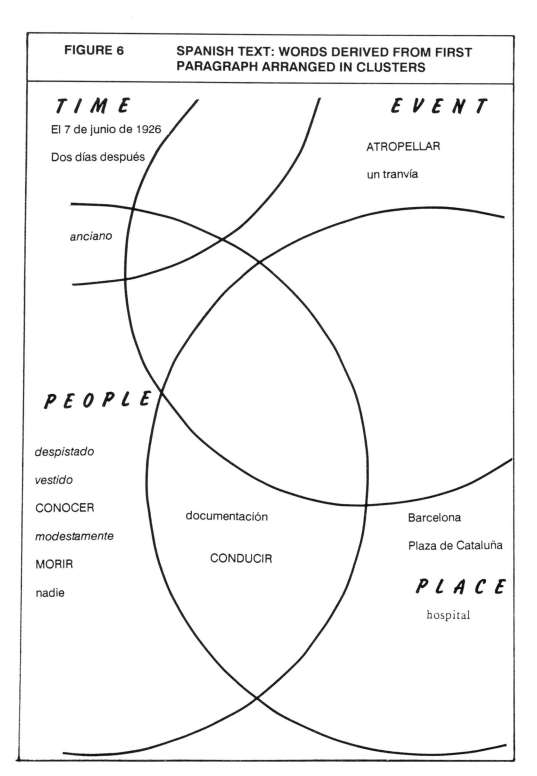

FIGURE 6   **SPANISH TEXT: WORDS DERIVED FROM FIRST PARAGRAPH ARRANGED IN CLUSTERS**

T I M E

El 7 de junio de 1926

Dos días después

anciano

E V E N T

ATROPELLAR

un tranvía

P E O P L E

despistado

vestido

CONOCER

modestamente

MORIR

nadie

documentación

CONDUCIR

Barcelona

Plaza de Cataluña

P L A C E

hospital

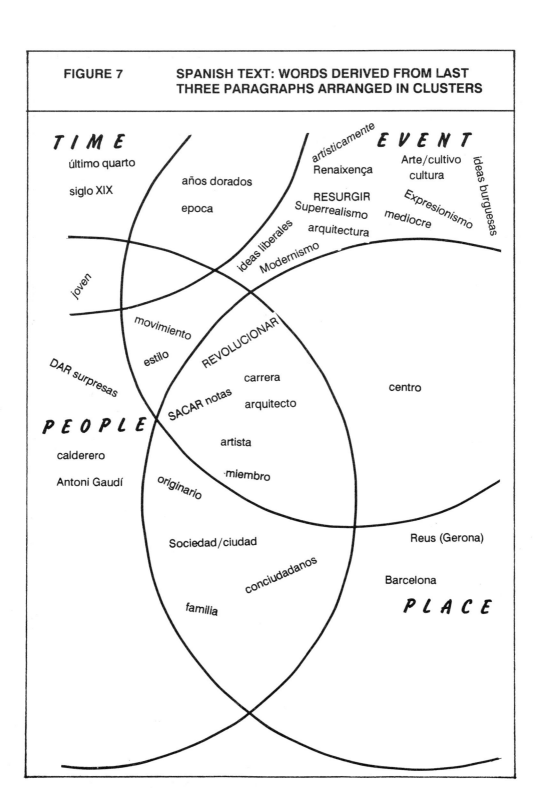

FIGURE 7   SPANISH TEXT: WORDS DERIVED FROM LAST THREE PARAGRAPHS ARRANGED IN CLUSTERS

TIME
último quarto
siglo XIX
años dorados
epoca

EVENT
artísticamente
Renaixença
Arte/cultivo
cultura
RESURGIR
Superrealismo
Expresionismo
mediocre
ideas burguesas
ideas liberales
arquitectura
Modernismo

joven
movimiento
estilo
REVOLUCIONAR
DAR surpresas
SACAR notas
carrera
arquitecto
centro

PEOPLE
calderero
Antoni Gaudí
artista
·miembro
originario

Sociedad/ciudad
Reus (Gerona)
conciudadanos
Barcelona

familia

PLACE

TABLE 12	SPANISH TEXT: EXAMPLES OF SEMANTIC NETWORKS				
	makes things	helps people	creative	self-employed	accepted member of society
arquitecto	sí		sí	sí	sí
artista	sí		sí	sí	?
calderero	sí			sí	no
carpintero	sí		sí		sí
medico		sí		sí	sí
policía		sí			sí

TABLE 13	SPANISH TEXT: EXAMPLES OF COLLOCATION POSSIBILITIES (X for subject, Y for object)			
	ser humilde	revolu-cionar	resurgir	ser el precursor
arquitecto		X		X
calderero	X			
movimiento		a Y	X	de un Y
sociedad		a Y		
familia	X			
cultura		a Y	X	

Word clusters, grids, and cloze technique

ful sets and suggest how the learner's knowledge of relevant semantic fields and possible collocations might be developed further. Each of the word clusters and grids can be taught, explored and tested by a variant of cloze technique. For example, after a cluster has been created, the teacher can cover over one of the elements and the learner has to use the skills required for cloze to work out what the missing element is.

The word clusters derived from the sample texts

In the case of the Spanish text, we have used two clusters, one for each section of the text; for the French text we have also provided two clusters but have further subdivided them into two sections to illustrate the different stages of the narrative. Had we taken the full German text (as given on pp.61f.) we might have used one or other of these devices, separate clusters, or one cluster divided.

Group work based on word clusters and grids

This suggests an interesting variant for use at the end of the chain of exercises. The teacher might divide the class into two groups and have each group work on separate sections of the text. This means that each group would end up with part of the information, yet that part would be quite coherent. The information might be exchanged at the end of the chain of exercises through a role play exercise, such as a court-case for the French text, or an interview for the German and Spanish texts. Productive oral work of this kind will have first-order authenticity since real information will be shared and reactions to the information elicited.

(iii) Developing the skill of using vocabulary, world knowledge and discourse knowledge to create a telegraphic text

Using grids to create telegraphic discourse

With clusters and grids of the kind illustrated in Figures 1-7 and Tables 5-13, learners now have the materials from which to create telegraphic texts. This might best be done by laying out the information from the clusters in linear form, with headings that match

104

Qui?	Quoi?	Où?	Quand?	Comment?
	incendie ravager	Besançon bâtiment	En avril 1985	
gamins	jouer	cage d'escalier		habituellement
	fumée épaisse envahir	cage d'escalier		
C.Tournier et deux autres habitants	pénétrer	immeuble		
	frayer un passage	->trappe de secours		
	trappe de secours condamnée			
Camille Tournier	pénétrer	->appartement		
pompiers	évacuer 27 enfants			échelle
C.T.	intoxiqué			fumée épaisse
	coeur faiblissant			
	hospitalisé			
	opération			
	perdre emploi			

TABLE 14   FRENCH EXAMPLE: ARRANGEMENT OF VOCABULARY TO PRODUCE TELEGRAPHIC TEXT

TABLE 15	GERMAN TEXT: ARRANGEMENT OF VOCABULARY TO TO PRODUCE TELEGRAPHIC TEXT			
Wer?	**Was?**	**Wo?**	**Wann?**	**Wie?**
Gerda und Erika Zwillinge	geboren	Berlin-Karlshorst	7 Juli 1939	
Gerda	kommen	-> Kranken-haus	1943, während der Bomben-nächte	mit Lungen-entzündung
Gerda	4 Jahre alt.			
Gerda	evakuiert	->Leipzig	eines Nachts	mit allen anderen Patienten
Gerda	Namens-bändchen verlieren	beim Transport		
Gerda	kommen	->Waisen-haus in Leipzig		
Gerda	kommen	->Pflege-familie	später	
Gerda	ziehen	-> Augsburg	1978	
Erika	bleiben	Berlin		
Eltern	Gerda		1943 Jahrelang	mit Hilfe suchen des Roten Kreuzes

TABLE 16   SPANISH TEXT: ARRANGEMENT OF VOCABULARY TO PRODUCE TELEGRAPHIC TEXT

From the first cluster (Figure 6) we get:

¿Quién?	¿Qué?	¿Dónde?	¿Cuándo?	¿Cómo?
anciano despistado	atro-pellar	Plaza de Cataluña, Barcelona	el 7 de junio de 1926	por un tranvía
	conducir	-> hospital		
nadie	conocer			
	ident-ificar		dos días después	
A. Gaudí	morir		poco después	

From the second cluster (Figure 7) we get:

¿Quién?	¿Qué?	¿Dónde?	¿Cuándo?	¿Cómo?
A. Gaudí Arquitecto	revolucionar a la sociedad catalana			artísticamente
El joven Gaudí	comenzar a dar sorpresas a sus conciudadanos XIX.		último cuarto del siglo	
	sacar notas bastante mediocres		en su carrera de arquitectura	

Developing the telegraphic text: morpho-syntax

the focal points of the sets: WHO?, WHAT?, WHERE?, WHEN?, HOW?. Tables 14-16 offer examples of what this process might yield when applied to our sample texts in French, German and Spanish.

In the case of the Spanish text it might be worth constructing a profile of Antoni Gaudí as follows:

Nombre	Gaudí
Ciudad di origen:	Reus (Gerona)
Familia	Caldereros
Carrera	Arquitecto
Vestido	modestamente
Documentación	ninguna

(iv) Developing syntax at sentence level

Learners can now use this material as the basis for constructing a text resembling the original. If they have used Post-its as suggested they simply transfer the elements of each sentence to another page and order them correctly, making whatever morpho-syntactic changes are necessary. Morpho-syntax (2b in Table 3) is crucial at this stage, and the use of Post-its allows learners to concentrate exclusively on this component. By way of illustration we give only the first few sentences of texts that might be created in this way:

French example

French text

Un incendie a ravagé un bâtiment à Besançon en avril 1985.
Des gamins jouaient dans une cage d'escalier.
La fumée épaisse a envahi la cage d'escalier.
Camille Tournier a pénétré dans l'immeuble et a frayé un passage jusqu'à une trappe de secours.

German example

German text

Die Zwillinge Gerda und Erika wurden am 7 Juli 1939 in Berlin-Karlshorst geboren.
1943 kam Gerda mit Lungenentzündung ins Krankenhaus.
Eines Nachts wurde sie mit allen anderen Patienten nach Leipzig evakuiert.

Spanish text
El 7 de junio de 1926 un anciano despistado es
atropellado por un tranvía junto a la Plaza de
Cataluña en Barcelona.
X conduce el anciano a un hospital.
Nadie conoce al anciano.
Dos dias después identifican al anciano.
Es Antonio Gaudí, arquitecto famoso.
Muere poco después.
Ha revolucionado artísticamente a la sociedad
catalana.

Cloze tests again - French example

At this stage cloze tests can again be employed as in the example below, based on the French text. The advantages of this approach should be obvious: learners have more confidence in using vocabulary which they are by now familiar with, and it helps them to focus on morpho-syntax at sentence level in a meaningful way.

Un incendie a (1)_____ un bâtiment à Besançon
en avril 1985.
Des gamins jouaient dans une cage d'escalier.
Camille Tournier a pénétré dans (2)_____ et a
(3)_____ un passage jusqu'à une trappe de
secours.

(v) Developing syntax above sentence level

Discourse: syntax above sentence level

The exercises illustrated here require the learner to combine simple sentences to form more complex structures; they are identical to Question 4 on the German Higher Level paper. The advantages that they offer, particularly at this point in a chain, do not need to be stressed. There are frequently different possibilities at this point, as the French example shows. As a last step, the original text itself provides a model for comparison.

French text

French example

Possibility 1
En avril 1985 Camille Tournier a pénétré dans un
immeuble à Besançon ravagé par un incendie où
des gamins jouaient dans une cage d'escalier.

Possibility 2

En avril 1985, alors qu'un incendie ravageait son immeuble à Besançon, Camille Tournier a pénétré dans les couloirs (pour sauver) des gamins qui jouaient dans une cage d'escalier.

German text

German example

Die Zwillinge Gerda und Erika wurden am 7. Juli 1939 in Berlin-Karlshorst geboren. Gerda war 4 Jahre alt als sie mit Lungenentzündung ins Krankenhaus kam.

Spanish text

Spanish example

El 7 de junio de 1926 un anciano despistado es atropellado por un tranvía junto a la Plaza de Cataluña en Barcelona. Se lo conduce a un hospital, donde nadie lo conoce. Dos días después le identifican, pero muere poco después.

4.6 Final comments

In this chapter we have dealt with the various components of the reading and writing process in relation to the question types used in the Leaving Certificate examination. We have attempted to isolate the skills that learners need in order to be able to answer examination questions and have suggested practical ways of developing these skills using authentic texts as the source of input. We are convinced that this approach is not only far more stimulating but also far more efficient than simply giving learners exam questions to work on, which can be a very disheartening experience, especially for the weaker learner.

The danger of basing too much teaching on sample exam questions

However, we have also suggested from time to time exercises which closely resemble the examination questions. In particular we have attempted to show that it is possible to use cloze exercises in a variety of ways, and that a compositional exercise such as is found in the German examination has great value for developing skills in the creation of discourse above sentence level. Comprehension exercises were dealt with fully in Chapter 3, but it is worth mentioning here that like cloze exercises, they can be used at various points along the way, and might often be created by learners themselves.

Translation into the target language

Translation into the target language is a special case. It is a difficult exercise at any stage of language development. We pointed out in Table 4 that the components that need to be developed for translation are vocabulary and syntax at and above sentence level. How might translation as an activity be associated with the exercises we have developed in this and the previous chapter?

Using exercises outlined in this chapter to prepare for translation

Perhaps the single most common fault among learners is word-for-word translation. This creates havoc with sentence structure and also with discourse structure. In order to get learners to translate ideas and not words and to produce something which reads reasonably well, whether in Spanish or English, it is possible to prepare the ground by using the types of exercise we have outlined above. Learners might, for example, be asked first to compose on the basis of key words rather than translate. This would guarantee a coherent text, which might then be gradually adapted to match what has to be translated. Even translating the telegraphic target-language texts into corresponding telegraphic English can have its value: it can sensitize learners to the importance of coherence in discourse and at the same time can serve as a first draft of a translation of the original passage.

The activities discussed above require learners to take initiatives

Finally, it is worth reiterating that much of the work involved in the activities we have suggested is done by the learners themselves. Some of it is basic organizational work that has to do with developing vocabulary and grammatical knowledge. The most teachers can do for their learners in this area is suggest the frameworks they might use and the materials they require; the rest is a matter of the learners interacting in various ways with the target-language text or elements of the text. The kind of productive and creative activities that we have illustrated in Chapters 3 and 4 requires them to make frequent decisions about content and discourse structure. They may also be required to take the initiative in seeking out models for editing their work. And, as we suggested in Chapter 3, they may also be involved in the design of these activities.

The importance of developing learner autonomy

We argued at the end of Chapter 2 that learner autonomy is one of the necessary conditions for successful language learning. Developing autonomy equips learners to take initiatives that increase their exposure to the target language outside the classroom; it also allows the teacher to require learners to do much more processing of authentic texts on their own, which should greatly reduce the effects of the constraints mentioned in 3.6.

Implications for the role of the teacher

As far as teachers are concerned, one of the intended implications of this book is that they should function as a resource (among others) for information and support, rather than supplying everything that the learner has to do or think.

Suggestions for further reading

For vocabulary and grammar learning, see the relevant suggestions at the end of Chapter 3.

Interactive Approaches to Second Language Reading, edited by P. Carrell, J. Devine and D. Eskey (Cambridge University Press; 1988) contains some articles that elaborate theories of reading; while *Learning to Write: First Language/Second Language*, edited by A. Freedman, I. Pringle and J. Yalden (London & New York: Longman; 1983) approaches the development of writing skills from a number of different perspectives.

F. Grellet's *Developing Reading Skills: a Practical Guide to Reading Comprehension* (Cambridge University Press; 1981) and C. Nuttall's *Teaching Reading Skills in a Foreign Language* (London: Heinemann; 1982) contain many practical suggestions for developing skills in reading.